Additional Praise for *Basketball Junkie*

"An affecting and harrowing memoir."

—Tim Bross, *St. Louis Post–Dispatch*

"Herren . . . has written a *chilling* book."

—Gary Washburn, *The Boston Globe*

"I really couldn't put *Basketball Junkie* down . . . a fascinating book, a tale of our times. It is the story of a man who survived fame, drug addiction, and a host of hometown enablers. It is a story of every kid's dream turning into a nightmare."

—Bob Kerr, *The Providence Journal*

"An unflinching look at a life of wasted potential . . . told with such bluntness and heart that you can't help but root for Herren to stay clean."   —*Kirkus Reviews*

"Chris Herren's *Basketball Junkie* is the story of what happens when a town and a family pressure a favorite son to embody their dreams, which turn out to be his nightmare. If a book can be both anguished and celebratory, this is it. Herren's account of his descent into hell and back shows that beyond the bench pressing and the sprints and all the other prep work that help to create an athlete, in the end, character-building is the one drill that really matters."   —Madeleine Blais, *New York Times* bestselling author of *In These Girls, Hope Is a Miracle*

"What a story. If you read a sports book—no, any book—that sticks in your head longer than *Basketball Junkie* this year please let me know. This was a walk down a long, dark street to places that most of us have never been. Who knew there was a regulation basketball court in the ninth circle of hell? Fascinating."

—Leigh Montville, *New York Times* bestselling author of *Ted Williams* and *Evel: The High-Flying Life of Evel Knievel*

A Memoir

CHRIS HERREN
and BILL REYNOLDS

St. Martin's Griffin ▲ New York

www.stmartins.com

Design by Rich Arnold

The Library of Congress has cataloged the hardcover edition as follows:

Herren, Chris.
  Basketball junkie : a memoir / Chris Herren and Bill Reynolds.
    p. cm.
  ISBN 978-0-312-65672-0
  1. Herren, Chris. 2. Basketball players—United States—Biography. 3. Athletes—Drug use—United States. I. Reynolds, Bill, 1945– II. Title.
  GV884.H446A3 2011
  796.323092—dc22
  [B]

                                                                                2011002676

ISBN 978-1-250-00689-9 (trade paperback)

10 9 8 7 6 5 4

*To Heather, who never gave up, and
in memory of my mother, Cynthia Herren*

■ACKNOWLEDGMENTS■

I would like to thank the following, all of whom were instrumental in their own way to my recovery: Ray Tamasi, the director of Gosnold; Ray Lenihan, Andrew Hoffman, and all the people at Daytop; Chris and Liz Mullin; Kevin Mikolazyk and Joleena Tate; Skip Karam, Bobby Karam, and Jimmy Karam; Miller House; John Welch; Mary and Steve Parker; Chuckie Moniz; and Ken Gray.

I also would like to thank some of the people who took a chance on me when I was raw, vulnerable, and starting my business. The Fiolas. The McDonalds. Pat and Joe Sharkey. The Chrabascz family. The Bode family. The Holes. The Murphys. The Wells. Sammy Martin. And the Coffee House in Portsmouth, where much of the book was done.

And a public thank-you to my childhood friend Jeff Caron, and most of all, to my father, Al Herren, and brother

Michael, who never stopped believing in me even in my darkest times.

—Chris Herren

George Witte, who was my editor on *Fall River Dreams,* believed in this project from the beginning, always understood it, and made everything easy. No writer can ask for more.

David Vigliano, my agent for over two decades now, also saw this right from the beginning and his great instincts have never steered me wrong. David Peak of Vigliano Associates shepherded the book through the process, and has my enduring thanks.

And once again, Liz Abbott was always there for me, with her judgment, faith, and constant support. This would be a lesser book without her.

—Bill Reynolds

BASKETBALL JUNKIE

■PROLOGUE■

In the autumn of 1992 I went to Fall River, Massachusetts, a tired old mill town in the southeastern part of the state, to write a book on the city's Durfee High School basketball team.

The idea was to follow the team through a season, to examine what the team meant to the city and to the kids who played on it, to look at a high school basketball team from the inside out. I chose Fall River because Durfee had a rich basketball history; it was one of the few places in the Northeast where both the game and the high school team were deeply imbedded in the city's fabric, a place where the high school team still mattered in ways it didn't in most other towns.

My plan had been to focus on the coach, a local legend named Thomas "Skippy" Karam, who had once played at Durfee, who had coached there for over thirty years, and whose fate it was to be ending his great career in an America so different from the one in which he had come of age. But it was quickly apparent that the story was more complicated. At the center of it was a psychic battle being played out every day between Karam and Durfee's junior star, Chris Herren, a battle that was both generational and cultural.

With his teen-idol looks and his swept-back hair, walking through the corridors of Durfee as if he were the leading man in his own movie, Chris Herren was the embodiment of the high school hero, and he was already being recruited by numerous colleges throughout the Northeast. He was young and strong, destined to play in the biggest arenas in the country. Though only six foot two, Herren had an explosive first step and seemed able to get to the rim almost at will. He had swagger, he had style, he signed autographs after games, and he seemed to have the word *star* all but stamped on his forehead. He also seemed to define hip-hop, then the new teen rage, with his nervous energy and naked emotion, and with his street-cred, the way he would bump shoulders with one person while on the move to the next. He was always on the move.

High school basketball was the lifeblood of the city, had been since 1947, when Durfee High School won the Eastern Massachusetts title and a caravan of cars made the drive to the Boston Garden, communicants to a sacred shrine. Local legend claims that it was the first time the Garden had ever sold out for basketball, and when the Durfee band played the school's anthem the faithful stood up all over the Garden and sang along, many with tears in their eyes. Back home in Fall River others huddled next to their radios, living and dying through the static.

In many ways, high school basketball was almost all Fall River had back then.

Once, there had been money in Fall River, courtesy of the mill families that ruled the city like benevolent despots. At the end of the nineteenth century the Fall River Line ran opulent steamships daily from Fall River to New York City, ships described in newspapers as "floating palaces." In Fall River there was electricity, and telephones, and streetcars—all the amenities of a thriving city. A public library, a spacious boys' club, an armory, large public parks, and a showcase high school—modeled after the city hall in Paris and considered at the time one of the finest high schools in the country—were all built with private gifts.

At the turn of the century Fall River was one of the most cosmopolitan cities in the United States, with the highest percentage of foreign-born citizens. It had evolved into a group of ethnic neighborhoods that operated almost like individual duchies, with their own churches and social clubs. The Flint. Corky Row. Below the Hill. The South End. The Highlands.

But by World War II the seeds of the city's decline were being sown. Much of the textile industry was starting to shift to the South, and the Depression brought grim realities to Fall River. Few American cities were hit harder. By the start of World War II 80 percent of the mills that had operated in 1916 were out of business, leaving a plundered industrial ghost town, abandoned buildings, high unemployment, and the feeling that the good times were all gone.

Except for high school basketball.

There developed a mystique about Durfee basketball, a tradition that only grew as they won numerous state championships through the decades. It was there for everyone to see, on the walls of the field house. It was there in the dusty trophy case in the lobby, in the game program that started off with a history of Durfee basketball. It was there in the Greek chorus of older men, at the games year after year, forever arguing who the best players were in Durfee history, the best teams, as if 1947 were no different from 1993. It was there in the fact that the games had been broadcast on local radio for fifty years. Most of all, it was there in the city's memory, the palpable sense that the past and the present were on the same scorecard, the fact that there had been only two coaches in almost half a century, the fact that the game was passed down through the generations like an old family heirloom.

And no one embodied that tradition more than Chris Herren.

His grandfather had been a huge star at Durfee. His father had been a star. His mother had been a cheerleader. Three uncles had played for Durfee, one on a state championship team. His brother, Michael, had been the school's all-time scoring leader until Chris broke that record in his last home game. No one ever had better basketball bloodlines in Fall River.

Could you make this up?

No, you couldn't.

In so many ways, Chris Herren was as Fall River as the old mills throughout the city, those monuments to another time: tough, proud, intense, never backing down from anyone. More important, he was everyone's ticket to ride, as if everyone had a stake in his future, as if his success were their success, too. In the summer before his senior year in high school, the local newpaper ran a three-part series on "The Courtship of Chris Herren." His announcement of his college choice was made at a press conference covered by TV stations in Boston and in nearby Providence, Rhode Island.

Despite the mystique, the little secret about Durfee basketball was that so few of its stars ever found a second act; they were comets that quickly disappeared. Hadn't that always been the unofficial motto? Born in Fall River, die in Fall River. Wasn't that the great unwritten story, all the legendary high school careers that never had been able to transcend Fall River?

Chris Herren was different. His talent took him far away, all the way to the NBA and the Boston Garden.

So when his career unraveled, it was more than just an individual's fall. It was as if the city had fallen, too, had taken one more symbolic hit, as if no one was immune, not even someone who had once seemed to play with the basketball gods. There was so much shame. His fall was public, at least in Fall River, with its newspaper stories of court appearances. He had fallen so far, so hard. And, in a way, a small city had fallen with him.

After Chris Herren left Fall River in 1994, much of the mystique surrounding Durfee basketball went with him. Never again would the team be as good. Never again would the crowds be so large. Fall River was changing, becoming poorer, more minority in composition, with 16 percent unemployment. The

American Dream had left a long time ago and wasn't coming back. What was happening then in Fall River was a preview of what would happen in America in 2008; there was a sense that the bottom was falling out. There were more kids on the team who had grown up somewhere else, who hadn't grown up with the tradition. The long story of Durfee basketball was, if not over, certainly different, and part of it had symbolically ended with Chris Herren's fall.

There had been clues. In Herren's last two years in high school, he was walking on some emotional fault line, and beneath all the cheers and all the headlines, he was in the midst of a troubled adolescence.

Leo Papile, who coached Herren's summer AAU team and who later became the assistant director of basketball operations for the Celtics, once said that in those two years "there was no one better in the nation in high school as a combo guard. He could run a team, tough as nails, shoot the long ball; he had great instincts and feel for the game. He could run pick-and-rolls. He had an NBA résumé."

But I knew that Herren was more complicated than just a kid who could take the ball to the hoop. He never seemed able to sit still for long, always seemed to be fidgeting, radiating all this energy with no place to go. There was a moodiness to him, too—one minute he'd be off in some private world where no one else was allowed, face blank, eyes vacant, voice soft and indistinct; and the next he'd be animated, the energy back. One minute he could be full of adolescent bravado; the next he could be surprisingly pensive, as if there was some inner battle going on, his behavior hanging in the balance. For all his notoriety, he lived inside a personal cocoon, one that had little to do with the world outside Fall River. Every day more mail arrived at school for him, letters from innumerable colleges, letters he rarely opened. He was an indifferent student at best, often leaving school in the afternoon without any books. He didn't read much. He hadn't seen a movie since watching *Hoosiers* when he was twelve years old. He watched little television, and had few interests outside of basketball and talking on the phone to either his friends or a number of admiring girls.

"Chris was always a star," said one of those girls, a Durfee cheerleader.

Star he was.

But a kid, too.

I got to know him very well in the time I spent in Fall River writing the book that was published as *Fall River Dreams*. I gave him countless rides. We played countless H-O-R-S-E games. We spent endless hours talking. I knew about his drinking, even went to a party one night. He came to trust me, to allow me into his world. That was no small thing for someone who rarely let anyone in.

Then again, I wasn't his coach. I wasn't his teacher. I was the writer of a book that, to him and to all the other kids on the team, had become little more than an abstraction, something to be published in some undetermined future, something that was never real. Until, of course, it was.

At one point, when the book was almost finished, I made him read a couple of parts that I believed to be particularly sensitive, because he was seventeen years old and I didn't want him to be blindsided.

"What's so sensitive?" he asked.

"How about the fact that you drink too much, and do no work in school, and every other word out of your mouth is 'fuck'?"

"Oh, I don't give a fuck about any of that," he said dismissively.

In fact, he only objected to one thing that I showed him, one thing that was so insignificant, his concern seemed almost comical.

It was an impromptu, profanity-laced speech he'd made to his teammates in the locker room minutes before a big game, one he ended by saying, "Let's just go out and fuckin' play like fucks and fuck them up."

"You see that last sentence?" he said, all of a sudden sounding like a young kid asking for a favor. "Can you change 'fuckin' play like fucks and fuck them up,' to 'fuckin' play like animals and fuck them up'?"

Yeah, Chris, I could.

He seemed to live exclusively in the present tense, to the point that he didn't even have a driver's license, even though he was more than a year over the eligible age, and didn't every high school kid want a driver's license?

"I don't want it," he said. "I don't need it."

"What do you mean you don't need it?" I asked one day.

"Everywhere I want to go, somebody will take me," he said.

Herren was different. Not playacting different, like many high school kids, trying on roles to see what fit. Really different. He didn't own a sport jacket. He had forgotten to sign up to take the SATs. He was forever late to school, even though he lived about three blocks away, and when Karam called him on it, he said that his parents left early for work and he didn't have an alarm clock. For away games he would show up to the bus without the gym bag that had his uniform in it, secure in the knowledge that one of his younger teammates would bring it on the bus for him.

Yet I saw a compassionate side to him, too. He was never better than when he was with young kids at the Boys and Girls Club, fooling around with them, playing table games, shooting baskets, making them feel comfortable. One time a sophomore, one of only two black kids on the team, had played a horrible game in a Durfee loss, and was close to distraught afterward. On the way out of the locker room, Chris put his arm around him, and he walked out with him to the bus, talking words of encouragement to him the entire time.

"There's no one like Chris," his teammate Jeff Caron said one day. "He only cares about what's right in front of him. The school could be burning down, but if there were two ants going across the floor he would be looking at them, asking you which one you thought was going to get to the other side of the floor first, wanting to bet on one of them. Everyone else would be running to get out of the building, and he would be watching those two ants.

"The whole family's different. I used to love going over there when I was younger. The house was always open, people coming and going. My house is like a fortress. Alarms. Bars on the windows. The Herrens' is just the opposite. Michael's always giving his car to his friends and then forgets about it. You ask him where his car is and he has no idea. They're all like that. You can't not like the Herrens. It's like they don't care about what most people care about."

No one could have predicted Chris Herren's future after he left Durfee and *Fall River Dreams* came out. In his senior year, Chris broke his brother's all-time Durfee scoring record, was a McDonald's All-American, was courted in his home by Jim Boeheim of Syracuse and John Calipari of the University of Massachusetts, and was recruited by Rick Pitino. His college career would take him from Boston College to Jerry Tarkanian and Fresno State, in the belly of the basketball beast, where Tarkanian once called him the "the best white guard since Jerry West." Then there were two years in the NBA, and stints with six professional teams overseas. Along the way he was profiled in *Sports Illustrated,* was the centerpiece of a story in *Rolling Stone* called "Hoops and Misdemeanors," in which he was described as what James Dean would have been if he had played basketball. He was also prominently featured in a Fox documentary on the Fresno State basketball team, and was an integral part of a story *60 Minutes* did on Fresno State.

Six years after he graduated from high school he was playing for the Boston Celtics, one of the few Massachusetts kids ever to do so. In one of his first games he had fourteen points and nine assists, and when the game ended he held the ball, his fist high in the air, as the clock wound down. The next day his picture was on the back cover of the *Boston Herald,* the local kid with a tattoo of a shamrock on his left forearm, a picture that seemed to come right out of central casting.

Nor could you have predicted that eleven years after I first went to Fall River to write *Fall River Dreams* I would bail him out of jail in Portsmouth, Rhode Island, after he'd been found passed out in the drive-through of a Dunkin' Donuts at eight in the morning, empty packets of heroin in his car.

Because, ultimately, basketball was only part of Chris Herren's incredible journey, and, in retrospect, nowhere near the most important part.

This is his story.

■CHAPTER ONE■

I was dead for thirty seconds.

That's what the cop in Fall River told me.

He said that two EMTs had brought me back to life.

"Just shut the fuck up," he said when I started to say something. "You were almost dead."

I was only a few blocks from where I had grown up, only a few blocks from B.M.C. Durfee High School, where there was a banner on the wall saying I was the highest scorer in Durfee history. I had gone off the street near the cemetery where Lizzie Borden was buried, Oak Grove. Maybe the worst thing was that I had just driven through Fall River for a couple of miles in a blackout, a ride I don't remember to this day. When the EMTs found me there was a needle in my arm and a packet of heroin in the front seat.

It was only about two in the afternoon, but I had been going at it heavy since early in the morning. I had put my seven-year-old daughter, Samantha, in the car like I did every morning after my wife, Heather, went to work. We drove through the nice suburban neighborhood in Portsmouth, Rhode Island, where we lived, and went to East Main Road, where the liquor store was. I bought a pint of Popov vodka, poured it into an empty water bottle, and started to drink. Then we went back home to wait for the bus that took Sammy to school.

By the time she was on the bus I had finished the pint, and I went back to the package store to get another one. Now I needed some money, so I drove to nearby Middletown, virtually on the Newport line, where Heather was working in a hotel. She had told me that morning that she would leave some money in the car for me. It was $40 under the mat in the front seat, and I started off to Fall River, about twenty minutes from my house, to meet one of my drug dealers. I gave him the $40, and he gave me five bags of heroin. I didn't take heroin at night. I'd shoot up at four thirty in the afternoon, just before Heather got home, so sometimes in the morning I'd be starting to get sick and needed more.

This was my daily routine, had been for about eight months. Put Sammy on the bus, go to Fall River, do some dope, and get back in time for when Sammy and my nine-year-old son, Chris, came home on the bus. That was my life, the only way I could function.

Sometimes I couldn't wait to put Sammy on the bus to go get my dope, because I was getting too sick, so I would put her in the backseat and speed to go meet a dealer in Fall River. I would make the buy and shoot up in the car while I was driving, Samantha still in the backseat.

How could I have done this?

People ask me that all the time. How could you shoot up with your daughter in the backseat? They can't believe it. Not surprising. I can't believe it either.

But that's what I did.

People think that when you're doing drugs you're high all the time, out partying. They think you're having fun. That's not it at all. You're not having fun. You're in hell. Without the dope I would be "dope sick," so sick that I couldn't do anything, couldn't even get up. I'd be in a fetal position. You have the sweats one minute, and you're freezing cold the next. It's like having the flu with restless legs, because you can't control them. They're kickin' all over the place. You also can't sleep more than fifteen minutes at a time. You wake up in the morning and there's no blanket, no sheets, the mattress is sideways. And when it gets bad, you want to ram your head into the headboard.

With the dope I could function, if you want to call it that. I could drive a car. I could mow the lawn. I could be something of a husband, something of a father. When I pictured a heroin addict before I became one, I saw someone emaciated, someone nodding off. That wasn't it with me, not in the beginning, anyway. I didn't do it to get high. I did it to function. By the time I got to heroin I was so far gone on OxyContin that the dope became medicine, something that made me feel good enough to be able to get through a day.

But there had been three times in the four months leading up to the day I essentially died when I overdosed, became that guy nodding off, the stereotype of a junkie. Because I was getting worse. Once, I had left Fall River at about eleven thirty in the morning and was driving on South Main Street into neighboring Tiverton on my way home, which was maybe ten minutes away, and I couldn't keep my eyes open. I nodded off, woke up by the side of the road about two and half hours later with one of my feet out the door. Another time I passed out in a house in Fall River with four other people there, and they were so scared that I was going to die they called 911. But I came out of it, and was walking out the door while the police were coming up the sidewalk.

My body was breaking down, but I didn't stop.

That's the fucked-up world you're in. Someone will OD on something they got from a particular dealer, and everyone else goes to that dealer because he's obviously got some great stuff.

So by the time I was in Fall River that June day, the heroin on top of the vodka must have put me under, because the next thing I remember was the cop talking to me on the way to Charlton Hospital, the same hospital where my mother had died three years earlier. And all I could think of was that my kids were going to see this on the news, and that I was going to go to jail, and that I was in trouble again. That this was going to be one more horror show, complete with more headlines and more TV spots.

A similar thing had happened four years earlier. I had passed out in a Dunkin' Donuts drive-through window at eight in the morning virtually around the corner from my house. I had been arrested, it had been all over the media, and it had ended my basketball career. I had come home from a CBA team in South Dakota, trying to get back to the NBA after several years of playing overseas, trying for one last shot, trying to salvage my career.

But this was worse.

I had no money.

Basketball was over.

I had no job.

My two kids were older now, nine and seven, old enough to know what was on the news. Old enough for their friends to know what was on the news.

Heather was eight months pregnant.

When I got to the hospital I was more drunk than high. The nurses were staring at me. They all knew who I was, and I wasn't a pretty sight. I didn't have any insurance, so the hospital wasn't going to admit me. I was in the emergency room, and I was thinking of ways to kill myself, because I had no hope. That was gone, had been gone for a while. I couldn't stop sweating because all the opiates were sucked out of my body after a shot of Narcan, which immediately brings on withdrawal.

Eventually, a nurse came over to me, a Mrs. Reid. She said she had known my mother, and that her husband had been a big Durfee fan, had watched the games with Mr. Karam's brother Bob (known as "Boo Boo").

"Where are you going?" she asked me.

"I don't know."

"Come sit with me."

I broke down, and then my older brother, Michael, whom I'd called, walked in. He was crying, too.

"We're going to figure this out," Mrs. Reid said to me.

They got me into the hospital.

The worst thing was calling Heather, and the surprising thing was that she wasn't angry. Or maybe it wasn't that surprising. We were way beyond anger by this point. We had been married for nine years, but I had known her since the sixth grade, when I met her at a playground in Somerset, just across the river from Fall River. She was by far the cutest girl I had ever seen, and from the start I was in love with her, even though I put gum in her hair that day. That should have been the first red flag for her.

We were always close, and all through high school we would go out for a while, then we'd break up, but we'd always get back together. We were never really in a boyfriend-girlfriend situation, because I was in no way ready for that back then. But we were in each other's lives. She was Heather Gray then, and came from a much more stable family situation than I did, and she watched the chaos of my life from the sidelines. She knew my world was spinning. But with her I lived a different life. She never cared about my basketball, and I liked that. With her I wasn't a basketball player. We went to proms together. She was a homecoming queen, a cheerleader, a star. We took different roads many, many times as kids. But somehow, some way, we always reconnected.

We got married in Fall River the summer before my senior year at Fresno State. Heather was pregnant, and there was no way in the world I wasn't going to marry her. Our son, Christopher, was born the following March.

By that afternoon in 2008, though, there had been so much heartbreak, so much horror, so much hell. There had been days living in the dark because the electricity had been turned off and we didn't have the money to turn it back on. There had been times when we had run out of heating oil and I would take a red gasoline can to the nearby Mobil station, fill it with diesel fuel for ten bucks, and trick the oil burner into starting again. There had been many times when Heather had thrown me out, telling me it was really over this time, that she couldn't live this way anymore, and I would end up in some fleabag motel in nearby Newport for a few days. Then the money would run out and I would sleep in my car, until finally she would feel sorry for me and take me back and then it would start all over again, all the lies and betrayals, the false promises and the squandered chances. This is how we lived. We were always trying to hide the ugly reality from the kids, even when they were sitting in the dark and the TV didn't work and it was cold.

I would steal money from Heather, and then tell her she was crazy when she called me on it. I'd tell her she should go to a doctor and get some help, that she was losing it. I'd be screaming at her. She would find needles and show them to me.

"You're fuckin' crazy!" I'd yell. "They're old ones. What's the matter with you? You really should get some help."

I lied to her. I lied to everybody. I would do anything to keep my lie going, to get the dope that would get me through the day—until the next day, when I had to do it all over again because without it I couldn't do anything. And by the end, all Heather wanted to do was get through the day, too.

"What's this, Chris?" she'd ask, coming back from the mailbox with an overdue bill. "You said you paid this."

And it would all start again.

We bounced check after check, going through thousands of dollars in late fees and penalties. She would sit in front of her computer and shake as she went through our accounts, looking at the money that was no longer there, or that was far less than what it was supposed to be, the numbers always going down, until there were no more numbers.

So by the time she found out what had happened, she really wasn't surprised. She knew I was sick. She knew I needed help, the kind of help she couldn't give me.

How bad was I?

About a month earlier I had been at a drug dealer's house in Fall River.

"Chris, this is real strong stuff," he said. "So go easy."

I didn't go easy.

When I woke up I had one black eye and the other was swollen shut. Seems the dealer had been so afraid I was going to die that he kept hitting me in the face to wake me up. Yet when he drove me home I bought ten more bags of the stuff that had almost killed me. That's how fucked up I was.

At the hospital there were women I had gone to high school with who were now nurses coming in to see me. Chuckie Moniz, who had grown up with my father, and who had functioned as one of my unofficial uncles, always around, always doing favors for me, was in the room. There were TV trucks outside ready to put the story on the eleven o'clock news. I had a security guard outside my room.

I was there for five days, but I don't remember a whole lot of it.

I eventually got into Star, a detox facility in Fall River just down the street from Durfee. It was June 2008 and the Celtics were playing the Lakers in the NBA finals. Seven years earlier I had been playing for the Celtics, making roughly $450,000 a year. Seven years earlier I had been in the middle of some childhood fantasy—at least that was the perception—and now I was sitting in a detox center and watching the Celtics on television. No one had to tell me how far I'd fallen, what I had lost. It was right there on the TV in front of me. I didn't have a quarter to use the phone. I didn't have a job, or any real hope of getting one. All my money was gone. And I was too wrapped up in my own addiction to see my own reality.

There was another kid from Fall River there and he had a plan. Star was on the second floor and there was an outdoor patio where you could smoke. He had a girlfriend, and she was going to put some dope inside a tennis ball and throw the ball up onto the patio when we were out there.

I was thirty-two years old, I had two kids and a wife who was nearly eight months pregnant, and I thought that was a good plan.

■CHAPTER TWO■

I never played a basketball game for fun in my life.

I played because I was expected to, because I had to.

And I can't remember when basketball wasn't there.

It was always there.

From the time I started Milliken League in Fall River as a young kid, basketball was never just a game. You had to win. I would sit in school on the day of a game, eight, ten years old, and I would have butterflies in my stomach. I had to win, because you didn't want to go back to my house if you lost. That was the way it was in my family. My brother, Michael, had never lost in Milliken League. His team won eighty-something games in a row. Then I started losing. Not all the time, certainly. My team still won championships, but there were losses in between, and we weren't programmed to deal with losing in my house. Winning is easy. Losing is not. I would come home after a loss and sometimes my father would tap my head, or pat me on the ass.

"Get him next time," he'd say.

Another time it would be different.

"You didn't do this; you didn't do that," he'd say. "You've got to be tougher."

But my dad wasn't your typical Little League parent. If Michael or I didn't play well, or didn't win, it was never the coach's fault. It was our fault. No one else's. He wasn't out there in the driveway coaching me, pushing me. He was never like that. His problem with me came when he thought I wasn't into the game mentally, when my attitude wasn't right. When I didn't play hard enough. When I didn't step up to take the big shot. When I seemed out of it. That's when he was tough on me.

I knew as a young kid that basketball was real important. I felt pressure right off the bat. Milliken League was crazy. There would be headlines in the Fall River *Herald News,* "Herren Scores 36 as Karam's Win," and this was a kid's league, elementary school. I had to win, and I had to score points, and that was just the way it was. I never liked it. I was a fragile kid, a nervous kid. I wasn't very good in school. But the expectations were always there. I was living in the shadow of a very accomplished brother. Michael was five years older, so when he was twelve and already on his basketball journey, mine was starting, too, whether I liked it or not.

Michael loved it.

Me?

I hated it.

It was intense. People were constantly yelling and screaming.

My father coached the team. The team, called Karam's, was owned by Boo Boo Karam, who owned a lot of things in the city. Fall River was real incestuous; the same few people controlled everything, had all the juice. Basketball was the focus of my house. I didn't have toys when I was a kid. I had sports. You didn't say you didn't want to play sports. Not in my house. My father and brother used to get mad at me because I'd say I didn't want to play sports.

But when I was three I had a basketball in my hands. A basketball was my toy. I never sat around the house playing with other toys. I was outside playing a game, doing something to help me get better as an athlete.

People talked about Durfee basketball, went to the games. There was a lot of pride in Durfee basketball, and it was instilled in you early. You walked into the field house and the red banners were everywhere, honoring the state championship teams and the thousand-point scorers. There were big crowds, and you had the feeling that you were watching something important. You learned early that you weren't playing just for yourself, but for the city, too. From a young age I bled the Durfee colors, red and black. Basketball was a bubble in Fall River, a world unto itself. Some kids lived in a small bubble; I lived in a very big bubble.

Later people would say that the game seemed to come easy to me. Maybe so. I always had success, but that's not what I remember most. What I remember was that it wasn't fun. Fun was playing with your friends in somebody's backyard. Once you played in real games and they started keeping score and counting points, it wasn't fun. It was something you did, something you were supposed to do well. You had to win. Milliken League was a preview of Durfee, when I would sit there in school and get nervous. I had butterflies when I was eight years old, and I only had one thing on my mind. To win that fuckin' game. Because to lose a game meant you had failed, and that was ingrained early.

The other thing I knew early was that the beast was inside me. I was not going to play in someone's driveway and lose. That was ingrained early, too. In the fifth grade I would play in the schoolyard with my friend Kevin Mikolazyk's father, who was a teacher, and we would go at each other so hard you'd have thought it was going to end in a fight.

The beast didn't always come out. Don't play me hard. Don't talk shit. Tell your fans not to yell at me. Do all that and I was just another kid with athletic ability. Hit me, trash-talk to me, tell your fans to get on me, and it was game on, you against the beast.

I played Little League, and it was the same thing. I was nervous there, too. I was good at baseball, the best twelve-year-old in Fall River my last year in Little League, hitting something like twenty home runs in eighteen games. I ran very well, even as a young kid. In my small group I was the most athletic kid, and my mother's father, Charlie Carey, took me to batting cages, taught me how to hit. We called him "P," and he took great delight in me playing baseball.

My grandfather was old Fall River, someone who grew up during the Depression. No one had any money. He was one of eight kids, and his father, who had come here from Ireland, had been laid off from his job in a boatyard on the waterfront.

"We always ate," he once said, "but we didn't have anything. If you had a nickel in your pocket it was a big deal. You could go a month without having enough money to go to the movies."

The only thing he really had was sports. He was a three-sport star at Durfee, and one day one of the gym teachers took him and a few other kids to a grassroots tryout for the St. Louis Cardinals in a neighboring town. There were something like four hundred kids there, and he was invited to the Cardinals' minor league spring training in Columbus, Georgia—the first time he had ever been far from Fall River. That tryout led to another one in Springfield, Missouri, before he decided to come home.

"After I bought a train ticket, I had about ten cents left," he said, "so the only thing I ate from Missouri to Providence was a peanut bar."

He went back to Missouri later in the summer and played Class D baseball, the lowest level there was. But it was a job, as meager as the paycheck was, and back in Fall River there were no jobs. He did that for two more years before he realized he probably was never going to make the major leagues and came back home, eventually joining the electricians' union, seldom talking about his life as a professional ballplayer.

I didn't know a lot about this when I was a kid. My grandfather was a very humble man, never talked about himself. But Fall River was smaller then; it was like everyone's families had been there forever, and I had friends whose grandparents had known my grandparents, and they would tell me things. What a great athlete my grandfather had been. How my grandmother had been a cheerleader, how pretty she'd been.

I spent a lot of time with my grandparents because my parents were always working. In many ways it was like I grew up in their house.

But the standing around on the baseball field drove me nuts. I couldn't stand still. Baseball took too much time to play, and you could only spit in your glove so many times. You'd be out in the field and maybe get three ground balls in two and a half hours. I could hit, but I was an awful pitcher. It was like being on the foul line, something else I was never good at. I hated pitching, dreaded it, just standing there, everyone looking at me. It was the standing around that made me quit baseball after Little League. It was way too slow for me. I couldn't deal with it.

I even hated the national anthem before the games, having to stand there while it played.

That, too, drove me nuts.

It was why I hated school.

I couldn't stand to sit there, was always thinking up excuses to get out of the room. When I got older I figured out little survival strategies. Show up ten minutes late. Go to the bathroom. Go to the bathroom again. Anything to cut down on the time I had to sit there. Because sitting there was torture. No one had heard of attention deficit disorder then, but I knew I had something that wasn't normal, something other kids didn't seem to have. Because I couldn't sit in class without being in extreme discomfort.

"Chris is hyper," the teachers told my parents. "He has a lot of energy. Don't give him any sugar."

So no sugar.

And go outside and play.

No sugar.

And do more push-ups.

No sugar.

And go outside and run around.

That's how my ADD was dealt with.

I was about seven when I first saw Michael play. He was twelve, and already he was a star, being called the best young kid in the city. He was in a layup line and some older kids from Lafayette Park were in the stands giving him shit. Lafayette Park was a tough place full of tough kids, and they were acting like bullies, like they were tougher than Michael's team, and there was no way he was going to allow that. They were yelling at him, calling him names. Then the game started, and my brother made a layup. Without stopping he ran right over and cracked this kid. Beat the shit out of him. I thought it was awesome.

Michael was my first hero. Yeah, like every other kid in Fall River I idolized Larry Bird and Kevin McHale and the rest of the Celtics, as Boston was only about an hour away, just up Route 24, the entrance to which was so close to my house I could walk to it.

But Michael was my first hero. He and I were alone a lot as kids. Michael was very protective of me, looked out for me. If some kid was giving me shit in middle school and Michael found out about it, he'd be there the next day and then the kid would never give me shit again. Michael was big and strong and could scare people, but he couldn't have been kinder to me. He never hit me, never threw me to the ground, never wrestled with me, never did any of the things older brothers often do to younger ones. I always felt safe with Michael.

My whole world as a kid was very small, from Phillips Street to Durfee, something I could walk in ten minutes. That was Fall River to me. I knew that once upon a time Fall River had been one of the biggest textile cities in the country, and, yeah, there were old mills everywhere, but to me the mills were where you went for cheap sneakers. I didn't know any of the history. I knew the Lizzie Borden nursery rhyme, but I had no idea where she had lived and when she had lived. I just knew that Lizzie Borden took an axe and gave her father forty whacks, and when she learned what she had done, she gave her mother forty-one.

Everyone knew that.

It was part of being from Fall River.

And in many ways Fall River was its own world.

Providence, Rhode Island, was a half hour to the west on Route 195. Cape Cod was forty-five minutes to the east. Boston was about an hour away on Route 24. Newport, Rhode Island, was maybe thirty minutes to the south. So it wasn't like Fall River was in the middle of nowhere, but for me it could have been.

My grandparents lived across the street. My elementary school was just down the street. Columbus Park, where we played Little League, was less than a mile away. I could walk to basketball courts. It was a time when you could walk around freely. All the parents in the neighborhood knew you. Most of the kids I ended up playing with at Durfee I had known all my life. We used to dream about that as little kids, playing together at Durfee someday, and a lot of those dreams came true. We would talk about one day playing, and the girls we knew then would talk about one day being cheerleaders. I used to walk to Spencer Borden elementary school with Peter Suneson, and Kevin Mikolazyk lived around the corner. My mother and Jeff Caron's mother had been high school friends, so I had always known him. I knew Brendan Gettings and Dan Callahan from Milliken League. Peter Pavao and Eric Santos, too. We all came from pretty much the same area of the city, the North End. The North End was where the money was in Fall River, although in Fall River that's a relative term. But it was where the Highlands were, the big houses, home to the civic leaders, the section that began at the top of President Avenue.

Complete with a sign that said, "Welcome to the Historic Highlands."

We lived on the back end of the North End. It wasn't the Highlands, but it was still one of the better neighborhoods of the city. Our house had a living room, a kitchen, a dining room, and a family room in the back that had been put in when I was twelve. Before that the house had been small. The house was right on

Phillips Street, with no front yard at all. There was a driveway to the left, and a house squeezed in beside us on the other side. There was a backyard about the size of a postage stamp.

There were three bedrooms on the second floor, so Michael and I had our own rooms. On the surface it was all middle class, certainly trying to be. But our family was more working class, blue-collar. Just like Fall River was. My parents both worked, left early in the morning and didn't get home until six or seven at night. My mother worked for the phone company, and my father worked for the city in family services, before he got into politics. He was elected to the Massachusetts state legislature in Boston when I was ten years old, and he got there by outworking people and by hustling, not because he had any money or advantages starting out. He parlayed being a Durfee basketball player and having a sharp street sense into getting elected. No one ever gave him anything.

When Michael was young, my parents lived in the projects, but I don't remember that. In fifteen years they went from living on food stamps in the Fordney Street projects near Durfee to having their own house that had a garage with a hoop on it, and owning two houses across the street, one my grandparents lived in, and one my aunt lived in. By every standard of measure, they were a great success story. But they worked hard for it, and paid a price for it, too. Long hours. Stressful jobs. Being away from home a lot, to the point that I ate both breakfast and dinner at my grandparents' house. But the neighborhood was good. There were a lot of families, and everyone seemed to look out for one another, so if my parents weren't home I would go to Kevin Mikolazyk's house.

It was the perfect place for perfect families.

But that was the problem.

The families weren't perfect.

They were all twisted—some more than others. Even as kids we knew that.

We'd be playing at someone's house and the mother and father would start yelling at each other, things getting hot, and we'd say, "Fuck it; let's go somewhere else." So we'd go over to someone else's house, be out playing in the driveway or something, and the same thing would start happening there, and we'd say, "Fuck it; let's go into the woods and start fires."

Every Monday I would go to Peter Suneson's grandmother's house for meatballs with Peter and his father, but his father didn't live with him. Peter Pavao's parents were divorced. My house was no different from those of the kids I hung with, except my parents weren't divorced. Not yet, anyway. They hung in there when Michael and I were young, but there were problems.

And when your parents have issues, your issues don't get dealt with.

From the beginning, I didn't do well in school. I never liked it. I didn't get good grades. I wasn't a "grade kid." I had a couple of tutors for a while, but nothing really worked.

My basketball was always more scrutinized than my academics.

So let's see: basketball got you praise, and schoolwork didn't. What would you focus on?

By high school my report cards were rarely paid attention to. And at Durfee it was easy to make the D's look like B's with the computer cards they used then. Either way, I knew what was important. They weren't writing about my grades in the Fall River *Herald News*.

We all learned to tiptoe around our parents when they were fighting. As a kid it was embarrassing, but you didn't talk about it, because it went on in everyone's house. At least everyone I knew. We'd be walking over to Kevin's house after school and his father's stuff would be out on the lawn, and more stuff would be flying through the windows.

My parents had gotten married right out of high school in 1970 and had Michael shortly afterward, and it wasn't easy for them in the beginning. My father's parents had moved back to Alabama when he was seventeen and left him in Fall River, so there wasn't any money coming from that end. My mother came from a big family, so it wasn't coming from her side either. They were on their own. They both were working, they had a baby, and my father, who had thought he was going off to play basketball at a local college, found himself the head of a family at seventeen years old. He worked for the housing authority then, dealing with kids in the projects. My parents had been classmates at Durfee, the high school star and the cheerleader, but they were different, too. My mother was Fall River; all her roots were there. She had five older brothers, who all had played sports, and a twin sister. She had grown up in a tenement on Seabury Street in the center of the city near Ruggles Park. There had never been enough money, and my grandfather had sold his car to send my uncle Charlie to Colby College in Maine in the late 1950s, walking to work after that. He was the salt of the earth, my grandfather was. He never talked about himself. Once, when she was a kid, my mother found some of his old trophies in the basement, and when she brought them upstairs he told her to take them back to the basement.

My mother always was ambivalent about sports.

She had seen all the attention on her brothers and their high school careers. She saw how the brothers who were good had big shelves for their trophies, while the others had smaller ones. She had seen how there had been more focus on her brothers than on her and her sister. Girls in Fall River then were not supposed to play sports, were not supposed to go to college.

I knew as a young kid that she didn't care if I played sports or not. I came home one day in tears.

"What's the matter, Christopher?' she asked, concern in her voice. "What happened?"

"I don't want to play Little League anymore."

"You don't have to play if you don't want to," she said.

Of course I did; there was no way I wasn't going to play Little League in that house. But my mother came to realize that there were negatives about sports. She certainly thought there were more negatives around Durfee basketball than there were positives—she had seen the circus that surrounded Michael and thought it was crazy, way over the top.

My father had grown up in Fall River, too, but his roots weren't there. His parents were from Alabama, of German descent. His father had come north to work at the Firestone plant in Fall River. I never really knew him because as soon as he could, he went back to Alabama. My father had grown up very poor, had grown up "below the hill," in a section of Fall River that was full of tenements, and in many ways was very old-world. Most people who lived there worked in the mills. It was a tough place. You either learned to fight early, or you were a victim. My father was never a victim. Durfee basketball had been everything to him. He had been a very good player, one of the captains his senior year, good enough to be recruited by some small local colleges. He had idolized Mr. Karam, to the point that criticizing him was taboo in our house, and with Michael's success he got a chance to relive his youth all over again.

I loved going to my brother's games. The field house was always jammed, Durfee never lost, and Michael was like a force of nature. He was six foot four and tough as nails. He was going to make his team win, or die trying. He didn't die often. In his last two years his team won forty-six straight games and two state championships. He was a three-time All-Scholastic in the *Boston Globe,* and at the time the only other kid who ever had done that was Patrick Ewing, who went on to become an All-American at Georgetown and a Hall of Fame player with the New York Knicks.

Leigh Montville of the *Boston Globe* wrote a column about Michael after one of those play-off games in the Boston Garden:

The eyes couldn't stay off Herren. He was involved in every-thing. He was involved in the good, the bad. He was involved in the ugly. One minute he was scoring, clenching a fist to the Durfee crowd, yapping. The next minute he was committing a charge, clenching a fist, yapping at the referee, yapping at himself. One minute he was up. The next minute he was on the sidelines at the end of the third period, blood rolling down his face from an eight stitch cut across the top of his left eye from an elbow, unable to sit still as the trainer applied a temporary bandage.

"I've got to get back," the kid was yelling.

"Be still and I'll get you back," the trainer was yelling in return.

"Tell the coach to call a timeout to start the fourth quar-ter," the kid was yelling. "Tell him."

The kid ended the night with 14 points, only three in the second half. He ended with the eight stitches. He ended with a bunch of roses someone had given him in his hands and his mouth still moving.

"That's just the way I am," fifteen-year-old Mike Herren said. "I play basketball like a kid."

He paused.

"I am a kid," he said.

That was Michael.

No one wanted to win more.

No one cared more.

But I saw the negatives, too. How people from other towns hated my brother. How they would scream at him during games and how he would scream back at them. How he was a controversial figure at sixteen years old. How people would call the house and threaten him. One day my father answered the phone.

"If your son plays tonight he's going to be a dead man. We're going to shoot him," a voice said.

One night a bunch of cars came down our street looking for him, and parked outside the house.

It was nuts.

Michael once said he had been in three hundred fights in his life. Who knows? But I know he never backed down from one. We were taught to throw the first punch. That was the rule. If you were going to be in a fight, never get punched first. Our grandfather taught us that. Our father taught us that. We were taught at a young age that wolves win. I grew up knowing this. Be tough. Act tough. Be a wolf. The city fostered it. Families fostered it. That was Fall River.

And no one was tougher than Michael.

You know how two guys square off and one of them says "Fuck you" to the other, and the other says "Fuck you" back, and it goes on like that?

With Michael, you never got in that second "Fuck you."

———

This was the climate I walked into as a freshman at Durfee in the fall of 1990.

I was Michael Herren's brother.

I even wore his number, 24, the same number our father had worn.

I was supposed to be the next great Durfee player, following in Michael's footsteps, and a lot of jealousy came with that, even from some of the older players. When the season started there were people saying I was playing because of my brother, that I wasn't as good as my brother had been and never would be. I felt that all the time.

Then in one of the first practices I had my hands in my pants and was looking at the cheerleaders over on the next court when all of a sudden a ball hit me on the back of my head.

"Quit playing with yourself and pay attention."

That was my introduction to Mr. Karam.

Well, not really.

I always knew Mr. Karam. I knew him before I met him. I had gone to his camp as a young kid, so I knew all about his screaming and yelling. And his swearing. Although that never bothered us, because this was Fall River. Everyone swore.

Or as an ex–Durfee player said in *Fall River Dreams,* "There is an entire 'Fall River rap,' a language they've been speaking for thirty years. 'Fuck' is a verb, a noun, an adjective, an adverb, the all-purpose word."

And, of course, Mr. Karam had coached my father, my uncles, my brother. In many ways, Mr. Karam was family. At least that's what my father and brother always said. Even my mother loved Mr. Karam, because when she was in the hospital after giving birth to Michael, feeling ostracized because she had gotten pregnant in high school, he visited her and gave her a little baby outfit for Michael. She never forgot that.

He put me on the varsity as a freshman. No freshman team. No junior varsity. The varsity. Sink or swim. I started the first game, and if some of the older players resented it? Tough shit. That was Mr. Karam's attitude.

To us, he had been there forever.

He was Durfee basketball.

He had grown up in the Flint, the Lebanese section, where the streets are lined with wooden three-decker tenements. The old gray Flint Mill is still there, even if the windows are all boarded up. It was built in the late nineteenth century, back when Fall River was called "the Spindle City" and shipped cotton around the world. His father, Tanous Karam, had come to Fall River from Lebanon when he was twelve years old and was working in the mills two years later. Flint was one of the poorest sections of Fall River back then, and Mr. Karam lived across the street on the top floor of a triple-decker with no hot water, no bathtub, and rats all over the place.

"I would run upstairs and a rat would be running down," he once said.

But I didn't know any of this when I was a kid.

I didn't even know that he was from Fall River, or that he was Lebanese.

Nor did I know that he had been seduced by Durfee basketball as a young kid, just as I had been by Michael's games. Or that he had used both basketball and education to get to Providence College and a better life than his parents had. Or that he had played for a tough coach in high school who ran practices like it was the military, a coach who was toughest on the best players. I didn't know of the similarities between us. I only saw the differences.

But I knew that Mr. Karam was Durfee basketball, and that he had been the coach forever. I knew that everyone knew Mr. Karam. I knew that everyone in the city called him Skippy, no last name needed. I knew that he was loud, and he was tough. I knew that he was the show.

I also knew that I was afraid of him.

That first year I didn't say boo. He was sarcastic, had a lot of one-liners, and his voice could cut right through you. He was famous for that. Everyone had a million Mr. Karam stories. But that first year his one-liners were never directed at me.

We got along the next year, too. Later, he would say that was because I was quiet, never said anything, but I don't remember him yelling at me a lot, or getting on me much. Maybe that was because I was only a sophomore. But he was old-school to the max.

My first game was at Weymouth, a Boston suburb on the South Shore, and right from the beginning it was a total zoo. A couple of days before the game, Mike Dowling of Channel Five in Boston had done a little piece on me, how I was Mike Herren's brother and a new face on the Massachusetts schoolboy scene. I had begun dunking the year before, and the piece had video of dunking to the music of New Kids on the Block. So here I am in the layup line before the game, several TV cameras lined up on the baseline, and there's this whole section of kids screaming at me and singing a New Kids on the Block song.

The game starts and people are yelling and screaming at me.

"Overrated . . . overrated," they chanted.

"Your brother was better," they yelled.

"Herren, you suck."

"Herren, your brother sucked, and you suck worse."

"Overrated . . . overrated."

I was a complete mess. I felt that everyone was watching me, judging me, even those who weren't. I had all these thoughts running through my head. Was I really ready for this, or was I only playing because I was Michael's brother? Was I ever going to be anywhere near as good as he had been, and what was going to happen if I wasn't? I had been awful in the first half, afraid to shoot, afraid to do anything. Mr. Karam wasn't coaching. He had been suspended for something he had done the year before, and Bobby Dempsey, the assistant coach, who had once been a Durfee star himself and had known my father when my father was a kid, was the coach.

We're in the locker room at halftime, and Dempsey is telling us how rotten we're playing.

"And Herren," he said, sarcasm in his voice, "you played the perfect half. You didn't miss a shot. Of course, you didn't take any, either."

I got the message.

I finished the game with seventeen points.

That was the beginning.

Durfee was very big, with three thousand kids. The old Durfee, where my parents had gone, was downtown. It had been built in 1886 and had been a showplace, with all kinds of things high schools didn't have at the time, like a gym and an auditorium and a drill field where the boys were supposed to march every day. It cost a million dollars to build, a huge amount for a school at the time, and had a clock tower with bells that rang twenty-nine times every morning, in honor of B.M.C. Durfee, the son of one of the old mill families, who had died at twenty-nine.

That was the legend, anyway.

The new Durfee had been built in the late 1970s, and it opened to rave reviews. It was modern and spread out, and was supposed to be the new showplace. It had the largest school library in New England. A media center. A pool that could hold six hundred people. A field house to fit twenty-five hundred. A football stadium to hold over four thousand. A modern locker room.

But from the beginning it was criticized for being too big, too impersonal.

"I still get lost in this building and I've been here fifteen years," one of the guidance counselors said in *Fall River Dreams*. "It's not a friendly school. It's not personal. . . . There is a real shopping mall mentality, too many kids milling around."

My friends and I dealt with that by carving out our own little territory, a hallway on the fourth floor where all our lockers were. This is where we would meet between classes. This was our own little world inside the big world that was Durfee. The field house had its own separate entrance from the parking lot. It was called the Luke Urban Field House, after the guy who had coached Mr. Karam in high school. By the time I got there, Durfee had had only two basketball coaches in fifty years. The court was called the Thomas "Skip" Karam Court.

It was the next year that I enjoyed the most in high school. Jeff Caron and I were sophomore starters, and we had a good team, the most talented team I played on at Durfee. Steve Motta, the current Durfee coach, was the center, very tough and good. Corey Luz was an athletic wing player. Doug Pontes was gritty and wouldn't back down to anyone. And because I was only a sophomore, there wasn't all that much pressure. Like almost every Durfee team, we didn't have much size, but we didn't go down easy. We eventually got beat in the south sectional final at UMass Boston, when a kid from Brockton threw in a lucky shot at the buzzer. If we had won, we would have gone on to play in the Fleet Center in Boston, where the Celtics played. But it was a good year, a fun year, the last fun year I had at Durfee.

Because it started as soon as the next year began. The expectations. The constant recruiting. The pressure.

One day in the preseason I told somebody, "I can't deal with Mr. Karam anymore. He's driving me crazy."

What I didn't know was that the same day, Mr. Karam was

telling the same guy, "I can't deal with Chrissie anymore. He's driving me crazy."

That about summed it up.

Understand that I love Mr. Karam. He stuck by me through all my troubles, even going to court with me a couple of times in the last few years. He's always been there for me. The Karams are great people, forever loyal. I talk to him once a week now, consider him my grandfather. I would do anything for Mr. Karam. But back then we were like oil and water. Old-school. New school. Old values versus kids of today. Call it anything you want. But we were like a bad marriage.

Was he the easiest coach to play for?

No.

Was I the easiest player to coach?

No to that, too.

It was like we met at the wrong time. Once upon a time, his coaching style had been unquestioned. But the world was changing, and Mr. Karam didn't want it to. The first year he coached, kids brought their books to away games and studied on the bus on the way home. I didn't study at home, never mind on the bus. Everything we did seemed to bother him. The way we dressed. The rap music we liked. The way we talked back to teachers. Our lack of discipline. Our lack of structure.

Everything.

We didn't want to be yelled at, belittled. We chafed at authority. At least I did. And Mr. Karam knew no other way; for years this was the way he'd been coaching, and it had worked. His record proved that. Six hundred wins. Five state championships. Already in the Massachusetts Basketball Hall of Fame. It was the way Luke Urban, his Durfee coach, had been. But that style was never going to work with me. Not then. I remember one time he took me and Jeff Caron to watch the University of Connecticut team practice, and Jim Calhoun coached a lot like Mr. Karam did, yelling and screaming, old-school.

"Chrissie, could you play for him?" Mr. Karam asked on the ride back home.

"No fuckin' shot," I said.

He laughed.

He knew.

That was the day I asked Mr. Karam if his wife dyed her hair.

"Yeah," he said, obviously not wanting to deal with the question.

"What's she trying to do? Attract younger men?"

Jeff Caron later said that he wanted to jump out of the car.

But that was me at that age. There was no filter. Whatever I was thinking, I said. I liked to push people's buttons.

Looking back on it, though, I don't think anyone could have coached me those last two years of high school. I was too wired, too wrapped up in my own world. I couldn't handle any kind of criticism. I would lash out, try to get the last word in, and that would just set Mr. Karam off. He could have thrown me off the team a hundred times. My parents' marriage was falling apart, and that didn't help, and there were many nights when I'd be up in my room and they'd be yelling downstairs and I'd be thinking, "This sucks. Life sucks."

Michael was out of the house, and it was just me and my parents, who were at each other's throats.

Mr. Karam was always telling everyone that he couldn't understand me, that I had everything going for me, but in my world, behind all the games and the growing celebrity, a lot of things were falling apart.

He made references to the team's drinking on weekends, and that would drive me crazy, too. It was like he had spies all over the city, knew everything. He called us the Edgehill All-Stars, after the name of a treatment center, and he always had practice on Sunday mornings where he would make us run and run some more because he knew that half of us were probably hungover, which of course we were. But we still didn't like hearing it.

Mr. Karam and I would be going along fine, then something would set us off and he'd throw me out of practice.

He even threw me out one day when an assistant coach from Marquette had come to see me. Not that I even knew where Marquette was.

Then he found out that I wasn't carrying my own bag to the bus to away games, that one of the younger players always had it.

"Whoever has Herren's bag is a bigger asshole than he is," he announced one night after we all had boarded the bus, then told me that if I didn't start carrying my own bag I wasn't going to play that night.

It seemed everything I did drove him crazy. The fact I didn't wear socks when I played, didn't wear a jock. He would just look at me and shake his head, then walk away muttering something. It was as if we lived in two separate universes.

"Jeff," he said one night during halftime when we were at Somerset. "Stop throwing those alley-oop passes to that asshole."

I had been slumped on the bench in the locker room.

"Who's an asshole?" I asked.

"You are," Mr. Karam said.

"I'm not an asshole."

"Yes, you are," Mr. Karam said. "Trust me."

Another time we were on the bus after an away game, ready to leave, and we couldn't find Danny Callahan.

"Where's Callahan?" Mr. Karam asked, agitated.

"He went back to get his uniform," a kid answered.

Mr. Karam got more agitated.

A few minutes later Callahan showed up.

"Way to go, Danny," Mr. Karam said. "You don't get any rebounds and then you lose your uniform and keep everyone waiting. A great night. You're a pisser, Danny. A real pisser."

"Mr. Karam," I yelled from the back of the bus, "you know there's no such word as *pisser*. It's not in the dictionary."

"Sure it is, Chrissie," Mr. Karam said. "You look it up and your picture's there."

The worst moment, though, came in the middle of my junior year.

We lost at Brockton, and he was mad at me because I didn't shake hands afterward with the other team.

I wasn't emotionally equipped to deal with losing. It was like the end of the world. It was like I had failed, like it was all my fault, like I had let everyone down—my teammates, my family, the city, everyone. My brother had never lost. I wasn't supposed to lose either. And I knew that when we lost I'd go home to a dark house, as if my parents were in mourning. After we won there would be people over, drinks, a party. After losses it was like going home to a morgue. You didn't want to go to my house after a loss. You slunk home and hoped no one would be waiting up.

After the Brockton game I was going down the stairs that led to our locker room. Mr. Karam was behind me.

"You're the reason coaching sucks!" he yelled at me.

I went into the locker room and sat down on a bench, my hands covering my face.

"Learn to lose with some class!" he yelled.

"I can't," I said.

"You better start to learn!" he yelled back.

Everyone else in the room was quiet.

"I'll never be able to," I said.

"Grow up," he snapped. "Be a man. Learn to lose with class."

I muttered something Mr. Karam couldn't hear.

He came right over to me, put his face inches from mine.

"You better start to grow up, or you're going to be out of here!" he yelled. "You're real close to being off this team. Don't open your mouth again."

Mr. Karam turned and began walking away.

"Now you can go out and get drunk," he said over his shoulder.

"What do you mean by that?"

"I mean you better start to grow up," he said, walking away.

"Can I say something?" I said, my voice coming through frustration and tears.

"SHUT UP! . . . SHUT UP!" Mr. Karam yelled. "Just keep your mouth shut."

About a half hour later we were on the bus and going back to Fall River on Route 24. The highway was dark, not crowded. The bus was quiet. It was always dark and quiet after we lost, like we were coming home from a funeral.

I knew I had to apologize, but it didn't come easy. There was still a part of me that wanted to know why Mr. Karam had to be such a dick. But I walked up through the darkened bus and sat down in the seat behind him. I said I was sorry, and Mr. Karam nodded his head. That was the thing about him. He never held grudges. When it was over, it was over.

"Mr. Karam, do you remember when we came up here two years ago?"

"Yeah, Chrissie. You were a ninth grader. You were a nice kid then."

"You know, I didn't like it when you made that remark about us going out and getting drunk."

"You all drink too much," he said. "Don't tell me you don't. I hear a million stories. If I benched kids for drinking, we wouldn't have a team."

But he said it softly, and I knew the incident was over, that everything was cool again.

I looked around and said to the others seated nearby, "You know, my parents always said Mr. Karam was family."

I believed that.

In many ways I loved Mr. Karam, even back then. I used to wish I were a better player so that when colleges were recruiting me, they'd have to take him as an assistant coach if they wanted to get me. I was always stopping in to his office during the day and we'd joke around, because off the court he was different. Then I'd go to practice and it was like everything he said bothered me. There were days when I knew I was eventually going to get thrown out, but I couldn't stop myself. I know it wasn't rational. But I wasn't rational back then. I was just trying to get through the day. Maybe I was just trying to get through the hour. When I look back on it all, it was a very nerve-wracking time for me.

You couldn't just play basketball at Durfee. There were expectations, pressure. You had to win. You had to beat New Bedford, our big rival less than a half hour away, right down Route 195 in the direction of the Cape, because Durfee and New Bedford had been battling each other since the beginning of time, and if we lost it was like the entire city went into mourning. You had to beat Brockton because that was the other big school in our area, and they, too, were a great sports city, the home of Rocky Marciano and Marvin Hagler, another tough, blue-collar, gritty place. You had to beat the suburban schools because we were never supposed to lose to teams like that—we were Durfee, and we had tradition and toughness and they had neither. You had to win the state championship, because anything else was seen as failure. Those banners on the field house walls were the standard. That's what you were supposed to do, too. You had to win for the city. You had to win for all the guys who had played before you, and all the kids who were going to come afterward. That was just the way it was, and we all felt it. Mr. Karam, too.

And it wasn't fun.

Heather tells the story of coming to see me play as a sophomore. She was used to me joking around, used to me without basketball.

"It was like you had a different face," she said. "Almost vacant. So different. As if you were off in some different place."

A few years later, when I was at Fresno State in California, two people from Fall River were trying to do a documentary on me when I was home for the summer. It was never sold for broadcast, but I saw part of it recently, and watching it was like having an out-of-body experience. I already knew what the ending was going to be. My hair was dyed blond, everything I said was totally full of shit, and it was like watching a train that you knew was going to have a wreck right around the corner. At one point Michael was interviewed, and he said how I wasn't playing for myself, but for everyone who had come before me and everyone who was going to come behind me. That I was playing for the city and all the history and all of it, and here I was, this fucked-up kid with no clue to the horror that was in his future.

As I watched it I wanted to hit the Pause button and smack that kid.

Then I wanted to throw him a life preserver.

■CHAPTER THREE■

My first drink was Cold Duck champagne.

I was twelve years old, and Kevin Mikolazyk and I found an old bottle of it in my basement.

We got away with it, and that was the start. We didn't drink a lot then, but whenever we could steal a bottle out of someone's liquor cabinet we would go drink in the woods. Me, Kevin, Peter Suneson.

A few years later we would stand outside liquor stores.

"Hey, buddy," we'd say to a guy going in. "Can you help us out?"

Someone always would.

By the time I was a freshman, I was on the varsity basketball team and had a whole new circle of friends, older kids. So instead of drinking fruit punch with freshmen, I was going to keg parties. We'd be out in the woods somewhere, or maybe a half hour away at the beach in Westport, or behind some old ware-house, eighty to a hundred kids. Then we started going to Sune-son's basement. His parents were divorced, and his mother worked nights. We called it "the Speakeasy." On a good week-end night there might be thirty people there, our own world. That was serenity to me then, hanging out with my friends, drinking, completely relaxed.

Sometimes my parents would be up when I came home and there would be spot-checks to see if I'd been drinking, little tests that I always failed. I might get grounded for a while, but since they were never really home anyway, that never worked. They'd yell and scream and threaten to punish me, but usually by the next weekend it was all forgotten. I think they saw my drink-ing as something all kids did in high school, like a rite of passage, not that big a deal in the scheme of things. At least that's the way my father saw it.

But by then they had their own things to deal with.

They both were always working, completely stressed out. My mother was moody, always up in her room with the door closed. My father was always up in Boston, or else out at some political function. And he was a drinker. Not all the time. He was a binge drinker. When he wasn't drinking, he was fine. When he was drinking, he was negative about everything, sarcastic, angry, and at those times I learned to stay away.

I certainly wasn't the biggest drinker in my group. My friends used to get on me for never really finishing a beer, just taking three or four sips and putting it down, then picking up another one later. I was no angel, and I did my share of puking and all, but there were guys in our little group who were much worse off. Drinking really didn't do it for me. I drank to be accepted socially, to be one of the guys. I wanted to be just like them back then, because we all had grown up in each other's houses. They were like my family. I felt comfortable with them. I didn't like it when my basketball singled me out, made me seem special, different. So I would do anything to be like everyone else. With them I wasn't Chris Herren, big basketball star. I was just Chris, the same Chris I always had been.

I certainly didn't see the drinking as a problem then.

Now, the acid?

That was a problem.

That started when I was a junior, and we didn't do it all the time, because it wasn't around all the time. Nor was pot. Later, pot was everywhere, but I never really liked marijuana. I couldn't deal with the paranoia that came with it.

I probably did acid fifty times, and it was fuckin' torture. To this day, I don't know why I did it, because it was never fun. I guess it was the power of numbers, the power of the group. There'd be five of us, say, and three wanted to do it, so the other two would go along with it. We'd end up laughing at other people's torture, sick shit like that. It usually lasted about three hours, and in the end you'd be begging for it to end. The only good thing about it was that it didn't smell and get all over your clothes, so that when you went home you didn't get in trouble.

It was $5 for a tab, and if it was around we'd all do it, but we had some horrible experiences with it. One night we were in this tiny apartment on Bay Street and there were two Tasers in the room. By the end of the night the walls were drippin' and we were shooting each other with the Taser guns. You would never know when a shot was coming. It was vicious. We were tortured souls. I saw kids crumble on acid. They would break down right before your eyes, all curled up, wailing, begging for help, crying their eyes out.

You'd hear about bad trips, horror stories.

"Yeah, right," we'd say.

Then we started seeing them.

One night we gave each other homemade tattoos with razor blades. I still have a scar on my chest from that night. Another night I ended up hiding in the sand dunes at Horseneck Beach, with no idea what I was hiding from. It was starting to get scary.

In the fall of my senior year, we dropped acid in the woods out in back of Durfee, one of our favorite drinking places. Periodically, the cops would come and we'd all end up running through the woods to get away, except for Kevin Mikolazyk and Peter Suneson. They thought it was noble to stay with the keg, like it was some kind of fallen soldier, so they always got caught. I never got caught. I would run like a rabbit through those woods, and the other kids started saying that when the cops come, just do what Chris does, because he never gets caught.

But this night was different. We weren't drinking, for one thing. We were dropping acid. Just two months earlier I had been the MVP of the most prestigious AAU tournament in the country in Las Vegas, and now I was in the woods doing acid. Two kids lost it that night, and in many ways they never recovered. One of them was a close friend of mine, and he was eventually institutionalized. I had known him since Little League, and to see him lose it that night tore at me, because no one could do anything to help him. We were all powerless.

That night bugged me out.

I was done with all that after that night.

Or so I thought.

The recruiting started the summer before my freshman year in high school, when I was at the Villanova camp and on the last day someone left a new pair of sneakers outside my room.

The next summer the letters from various schools started coming, and by my junior year it was flat-out crazy. As a sophomore I was named an All-Scholastic by the *Boston Globe,* and the only sophomores to do that before were my brother, Michael, and Patrick Ewing.

I spent the summer before my junior year playing for the Boston Amateur Basketball Club (BABC), an AAU team run by Leo Papile, who now works for the Celtics as a personnel guy. Leo had started it in the late 1970s, and all the great players from the Boston area had played for it, everyone from Ewing to

Dana Barros, who became a longtime NBA player, and Rumeal Robinson, who starred on a Michigan team that won the NCAA title.

Leo was the best.

He liked to say that he lived in the bowels of basketball, and in many ways that was true. He was big and burly and wore his blond hair in a ponytail. His father had been a Boston cop, and there was no bullshit about Leo. Ever. He told you how it was all the time. He could walk into the worst section of Boston, into little gyms and rec centers that no white people ever walked into, and everyone knew him. He had flair, was full of charisma. He had started identifying the best kids in Boston when they were young and getting them into prep schools so when it came time to go to college they could pass the SATs. By the time I met him he'd been doing it for years, and everyone knew that BABC was the gold standard in New England.

Leo was forty then, and he usually wore open shirts with a couple of gold chains hanging around his neck. He had grown up in Quincy, just south of Boston, and had once played a state tournament game in the Boston Garden against Durfee and my father, so he knew all about the Durfee tradition. When he was twenty-five he coached a team in the old Eastern League, one of those leagues where guys play in little gyms and drive around in vans, old-time basketball. That summer he started an AAU team and took BABC to a few national tournaments. That whole AAU scene was just beginning, but four kids on that team eventually ended up in NBA camps. That was proof to Leo that there was real talent in Boston, talent that had never really been mined before.

That was the beginning.

For me, BABC was the first time I looked beyond Fall River.

Before I went to BABC I had played on a local AAU team coached by Jimmy Tavares. It was made up of kids from all over Bristol County, the county Fall River was a part of, and we traveled in a van. We were up at a tournament in Springfield, where basketball was invented and where the Basketball Hall of Fame is. There were ten of us, and we're putting on shitty uniforms, and I look over and there's BABC, six or seven guys, nice uniforms, and they're staying in a hotel for the weekend while we're going back and forth, all of us crammed into the back of the shitty van. Bobby Dempsey knew Leo, and one thing led to another.

"What about Herren?" Dempsey asked. "He belongs with you guys."

Right before I joined BABC we had played in a local tournament against them and I'd had a good game. I had also gotten to know some of the kids on BABC, and we used to call each other on the phone. But when I first joined them I was nervous. The kids were older than I was, better, all from Boston. Jamal Jackson. Carmelo Travieso. Casey Arena. Shannon Bowman. I was the outsider, the only white kid at the time. But I liked that. To be able to play with black kids, to be accepted by them, is huge for a white kid's confidence, because until you prove you can play with black kids, you are suspect in basketball. But Leo handled me perfectly. In the beginning he played me in spurts, got me comfortable, and built my confidence. He handled me like I should have been handled back then, letting me go along at my own pace.

"He doesn't care about how many points he gets," Leo once said about me. "He doesn't even care about how he plays. He only cares about winning. He only cares what the scoreboard says. And there was never any adjustment problem. My kids are all street urchins and Chris fit right in."

Playing for BABC was different from playing for Durfee.

For one thing, my game was different, especially the first year. I learned to cater to the older kids, to get them the ball at the right time, to fit in.

It was the first time I had been on a team outside of Fall River, and I loved it. The pressure was gone. I didn't have to be great. I didn't have to always play well, or we would lose. No one really knew who I was, and if they did, they certainly didn't care. I got along with everyone, and Leo was never a screamer. We often traveled to tournaments in three rental cars, to Virginia and North Carolina and around the east.

In a sense we all had something to prove, and Leo was a master at using that. We weren't the Gauchos or Riverside Church, the two elite AAU teams in New York, which were both well-funded and nationally known. We weren't the Road Runners in New Jersey. We weren't regarded back then as one of the big-time AAU teams in the country. They got all the attention, and

Leo never let us forget it. We were under the radar. But we were a team with a swagger, a team that was going to get down and dirty with you, fight you to the end. We had no egos. Instead, we had a collective ego. No one cared how many points they scored, or how many shots they got, or even about playing time. It was all about winning. It was all about accepting everybody for what they brought to the team.

We usually practiced two or three times a week in Boston, and Chuckie Moniz would drive me up and back. In tournaments we might play as many as seven games in a weekend. It always seemed like an adventure. The hotels. Life on the road. It was all new, and I loved all of it. No one knew who my brother was. No one knew who my father was. Not like in Fall River, where there were HERREN bumper stickers on cars because of my father's political career.

Or as Leo used to say, "Forget the name; bring the game."

We went something like 75–2 in the summer before my junior year, and more schools started to hear about me. My world was changing, even if it really didn't mean a whole lot at the time. It had nothing to do with my real life. My real life was right in front of my face. Forget visualizing the future; I couldn't visualize next week. I lived in the present tense to a fault, like I was always going to be seventeen and a junior at Durfee.

But my AAU success got me on the radar screen.

In the fall of my junior year there had been a story in *Eastern Basketball* in a section called "Middle Atlantic Prep Report." It was written by some guy named Tom Strickler, and it was about our BABC team. It commented on all the players, particularly our stars, Jamal Jackson and Shannon Bowman, then said:

Last, but certainly not least, is my favorite player, "Popeye." That would be 6-foot-2 Chris Herren, from Durfee High near Boston. "Popeye," as Papile aptly named him, could play the lead in *Bowery Boys, Boys Town,* or any other flick that depicts troubled lads or hard-nosed street kids. Let me emphasize that Chris is neither. He's just a flat-out feisty dude who plays with a scowl and a temperament that could scare Jason on Halloween. The more you watch Chris, the more you like everything about his game. I chuckled at first when I first heard of Big East interest, but after five games I believed. He punctuated his three-day performance with an alley-oop dunk. . . . I was surprised, then realized it was "Popeye." Nothing he will do could surprise me anymore. Keep up that spinach diet, kid. Welcome Big East teams, ACC teams, Big Ten teams. Here's "robo-guard II."

After that, the letters came to Mr. Karam's mailbox every day from schools all over the country, some in places I had never heard of. There were notes from coaches. There were brochures. There were pamphlets. Every Big East team. UCLA. UNLV.

"There must be twenty pieces every day and maybe two of them for me," Mr. Karam told the *Standard Times* of New Bedford. "The secretaries in the office say they're going to switch the name on the box from Karam to Herren. Kentucky, North Carolina, and Duke haven't contacted him yet, but just about everyone else has."

Mr. Karam was constantly after me to get those letters out of his office, take them home.

I rarely did.

I was too busy trying to copy somebody's homework in study hall.

Before the season started, Tom Konchalski, who lived in New York and was the godfather of the high school talent evaluators, had me listed as one of the twelve best juniors in the Northeast. He called me "White Lightning."

It's a funny thing being a white basketball player, because right from the beginning you're fighting racial stereotypes. White players are always suspect, always assumed to be not athletic enough.

White man's disease?

Everyone in basketball believes it, believes you aren't athletic enough, until it's proven otherwise.

So in the beginning, if you're any good, you're called "tough and hardworking."

Then it's "tough and hardworking who can shoot a little bit."

Then it's "tough and hardworking who can shoot a little bit and can pass."

By the time they say, "The kid can play," you're finally accepted.

In one of his reports, Konchalski had called me "the toughest kid on any block," and wrote this: "Right now he lacks the ability to score from the outside, and part of that is a macho thing, the need to always take the ball to the basket. But he has a tremendous will to win. If Chris Herren had been a Jesuit priest in the [sixteenth] century in upstate New York, the Iroquois would have cut out his heart and eaten it for courage."

I had no idea what he was talking about.

One night in my junior year, Leo brought Konchalski to Fall River for a Durfee game. The field house was packed, like it always was for a big game, and at the end of it, as both teams were going through the traditional postgame handshake, an opposing fan bumped Mr. Karam.

That started it.

Punches.

Bodies flying.

Two cops trying to break it up.

It was totally berserk.

Mr. Karam's jacket was off; his white shirt out of his pants. Two guys who were fighting bumped into me and knocked me to the floor. People were yelling and pushing, and just when it seemed like it was going to be a total zoo, it ended. But that was Fall River. That's how arguments got settled. No guns, no knives. The old-fashioned way. People whaling on each other, kids, adults, everybody.

A full Fall River.

In the beginning, getting the letters from schools was great, like being introduced to this big new world, to all the teams I saw on television. Now they were writing me letters. Schools like Florida, Wisconsin, Syracuse, Boston College. What could be better than that? There was something otherworldly about it, because at the time it had nothing to do with my life. My world was still only a few blocks. That was my worldview. My brother had a lot of interests. Ask him about politics and he'd talk for hours. I couldn't have cared less about politics. Clinton was president when I was in high school, and I didn't really know anything about him. Nor did I care. Michael would have given anything back then to have been able to meet JFK. I didn't know diddly about JFK. Michael was forever telling me I was so culturally deprived I couldn't name the Beatles. He said that so often that I finally knew who they were. But I always forgot that Harrison guy.

I didn't care about that either.

The only thing I cared about was my friends. Me, Kevin Mikolazyk, Pavao, Suneson, the guys we hung with, the inner circle. No one else was invited in. It was a small world, and that's the way we liked it. That was what I could control, what I felt comfortable with. I didn't care about baseball, or football, or any sport other than basketball. School was just somewhere I went every day. I rarely did any homework. I didn't have to at Durfee. I got by. That was enough.

The letters from schools don't really mean anything in the big scheme of things, although you don't know that at the time. When they start to get personalized, the game changes.

But I came to hate recruiting, to see it as very destructive to a kid. It puts you in an almost impossible situation. Ron Stewart was an assistant at Florida, and he came to see me when I was a sophomore. He was the first coach who came to Durfee. He was always there, and when I had to tell him I wasn't going to Florida, I felt awful.

The summer before my senior year, my world changed.

It happened in Vegas, of all places.

We were playing in something called the John Farrell Tournament, and it was the most prestigious AAU tournament in the country, the unofficial national championship. All the big-name coaches were there; it was the biggest meat market you can imagine. There's a sense of unreality about it, that all these famous coaches you've seen on TV a million times are sitting in the front row watching you play. Rick Pitino. P. J. Carlesimo. A who's who. And when it ended, we had won the tournament and I was the MVP.

After that, it seemed like everyone wanted me.

I had gone out to Vegas as one of the most recruited players in the country and came back as one of the true elite. One scouting service had me as the seventh best prospect in the country. Another said I was the best player in the country under six foot five. Pitino and Kentucky were now recruiting me, and Pitino had assigned Billy Donovan, one of his assistants, to watch over me.

The phone was always ringing, letters were always coming into Durfee. It was nuts. My brother and a couple of his friends rented a cottage in Westport, real close to the beach, a half hour from Fall River. It was like a party house. They had a sign that said "Waco North." That was my escape, a place where the phone didn't ring. If I wasn't off somewhere with BABC, I was there drinking my brains out. Two nights a week I played for Durfee in a local summer league, but after Vegas that got crazy. We played Taunton one night and this big football player laid me out in the game, and then wanted to fight, and Michael came out on the court threatening everybody, and the whole thing turned into a total zoo. I got thrown out and suspended for the next game. It was like the volume had been turned up on everything. The Fall River *Herald News* ran a three-part series, "The Courtship of Chris Herren." The first installment was an interview with Mr. Karam, who said that in all his years he had never gone through anything like this, and that he didn't try to pressure me one way or the other.

"As a coach, if you push him to a particular school and he doesn't do well or doesn't like it you feel responsible," he said. "I don't think it's my place. It's his life, his future, and he's the one who's going to have to live with his choice."

He said that I was the best he'd ever coached, something he'd been reluctant to say before.

"He's by far the best," he said. "I don't usually say those things, but if I didn't say that Chrissie was the best I'd be lying."

In the same article, Leo called me the best high school player in the country. He had also told both the *Boston Globe* and the *Boston Herald* that he considered me one of the top talents ever to come out of Massachusetts, someone who had the potential to have a "ten-year career in the NBA."

But none of that meant anything to me. The NBA was the last thing on my mind then. How could it be? I was a six-foot-two white kid from Fall River, a place that had sent only a handful of kids to Division I college basketball, never mind the NBA. Plus, my vision of the future was about fifteen minutes. The only goal I had was to be the best player on the court that day. Court to court. That was it. I wasn't playing to get anyplace. I wasn't playing for some far-off future. None of that ever registered.

The only thing I knew was that I was successful in the games I played in, even the ones in Las Vegas where the best high school players in the country were.

The NBA?

The very idea of that back then would have been nonsense.

The second part of the series was on the relationship between Michael and me, how he had gone through a similar recruiting process when he was in high school, and thus could give me advice. Michael also tried to set the record straight once and for all on why he had left Boston College, prefacing it by saying he had never really felt comfortable there.

"I left because my basketball career was in jeopardy because of injuries I had and because the media pressure was becoming stifling," Michael said. "Everything I did was in the paper, it seemed. I was eighteen, nineteen years old going through that. I wasn't a senator, someone thirty-five. I was still a baby.

"I want to set the record straight about those troubles. I do not have a police record. I lived life on the edge for a seventeen-, eighteen-year-old. I definitely did, but I wasn't the only one doing it. Maybe I shouldn't have been drinking as much as I was for an eighteen-year-old, or fighting as much. I shouldn't have put myself in those tough situations. . . .

"I'm not going to tell Chris not to go out and have a good time. I'm not going to tell him not to enjoy his high school experience. What I can tell him is not to test fate. If you test fate you're going to get burned. I tested fate a little too much."

But I already knew that it was all getting crazy, that there was no way I was ever going to be a normal seventeen-year-old kid in Fall River.

"Fortunately I haven't been in any situations where my name would be in headlines," I told the *Herald News*. "I've always had positive ink, but if I stub my toe, people are going to want to know about it. I had some friends at Howard Johnson's the other night who got arrested [for drinking]. I could have been with them, but I wasn't. If I were there, I'm sure it would have been in every paper in the area. I'm seventeen years old. I'm a kid and kids make mistakes, but I guess I have to keep myself out of those kinds of situations."

At the end of the three-part series I was asked what college I was going to.

"I'm going to Durfee," I said.

The *Herald News* wrote an editorial about it, praising me for living in the present tense, for realizing that you're only in high school once and making the most of it.

If they only knew.

Everywhere I went people were asking me where I was going after Durfee. It was endless, and it was like everyone had an opinion about where I should go.

I didn't like it.

I didn't like anything about it.

I wanted one school to jump out and grab me by the throat.

I was leaning more and more toward Kentucky. It was the school I was the most curious about. I liked Billy Donovan. Why not go to the biggest stage there was? That's how I was beginning to think as the summer wore on.

"Come on," Michael said one day. "Let's jump in the car and drive to Kentucky right now. Drive straight through and take a look at it when they don't know we're coming. See for ourselves."

"How far is it?" I asked.

"Who cares how far it is?" Michael said. "We'll get in the car and we'll stop when we get there."

"You're crazy, bro."

"Chrissie, the biggest decision of your life and you don't care enough to go find out for yourself."

"How far is it?

"Who cares how far it is?"

"I do, Michael."

"That's your problem.'

"I don't have a problem, Michael."

"Keep it up, Chrissie, and you'll have a problem."

"Not from you, bro."

"Chrissie, just remember who you're talking to. You're still the little brother. Just remember that."

So we never went to Kentucky.

We went out for grinders at Marzilli's instead.

One night we were playing a summer league game in an outdoor court in the middle of Harbor Terrace, a housing project in the shadow of the Braga Bridge that led from Fall River to Somerset on Route 195. That afternoon I had shot in the Boys Club on Bedford Street, one of the places I would work out during the summer, for Lon Kruger, the coach of Florida, and his assistant Ron Stewart. That night at the game, Stewart and Villanova assistant John Leonard were in one corner, Donovan and Wisconsin coach Stu Jackson were in another, and BC coach Jim O'Brien was in the middle. All around were TV cameras and photographers.

"I've never seen anything like this around here," Mr. Karam was quoted as saying in the next day's paper. "I've spoken to more coaches in the past few days than I did in thirty years."

That night, after the game, all the coaches went to T.K. O'Malley's, a restaurant in a small shopping center near Route 24 owned by Boo Boo Karam. So did Michael and his friends.

At one point, I went there to get a ride home from Michael, because I still didn't have my license, but I didn't want to go in because I knew the coaches were there. So I was sitting by myself in the parking lot. I was probably there for an hour before Michael finally came out. I didn't like the coaches coming to Fall River. It all felt bizarre to me somehow. I didn't mind playing in front of them at tournaments, but when they were in Fall River it was like my two worlds were colliding, everything closing in on me.

■CHAPTER FOUR■

The schools that came to my house for home visits that fall were Syracuse, Villanova, Seton Hall, Florida, Wisconsin, Providence, UMass, and Boston College.

By then I was completely sick of the whole recruiting thing.

The phone would ring.

"Is this Chris?" a voice would say.

"No, this is his brother, Michael. Chris isn't here."

I wanted nothing to do with it anymore. I just waited for the weekend to be with my friends and escape, shut everything else out.

Kentucky had backed out; it had come down to me and another guard from Florida, and Donovan had told me that the one who decided first was going to get the scholarship. I couldn't decide, and that was it. Kentucky had been the one that had everyone in Fall River excited. Kentucky was Rick Pitino, who had taken Providence College to the Final Four just six years earlier, and people in Fall River loved Pitino because Providence, Rhode Island, was just a half hour away. He had been the speaker at the banquet at the Venus de Milo in 1988 when Michael's team won their second state championship, something two thousand people had attended. I always sensed everyone wanted me to go to Kentucky.

But me?

It was like I was paralyzed; not just about Kentucky, but about all of it. It was nerve-wracking playing for Durfee and Mr. Karam, and that was just a few blocks from my house, never mind the thought of going off to Kentucky and playing for Rick Pitino. I might have been more intrigued with Kentucky than with anywhere else, but being intrigued and actually pulling the trigger were two very different things.

One night a friend asked me where I wanted to go, and I said I didn't know.

"I wish there were a University of Fall River," I finally said.

It was all too much, too big a decision, or at least a decision I was nowhere near emotionally ready to make. There were too many voices ringing in my head. Everyone had their opinion, and the only consensus was that I shouldn't go to Boston College, because my brother had gone there and he had failed.

I should go anywhere but Boston College.

I remember little about most of those visits now, more flashes of things rather than specifics. I remember meeting P. J. Carlesimo at Al Mac's Diner and bringing him to my house. Jim Boeheim came in and sat on the couch like it was his house, as relaxed as he could be. He was very low-key, almost matter-of-fact, and my parents liked him. Then again, they liked all the coaches, because they were all good at what they did. Sure, they're telling you what you want to hear, but there was nothing high pressure about it. They talked about the support structure, and their schedule, and how good they were going to be, and how they had no doubt I'd fit in at their school, and every time they left I could see myself going there. I liked all of them.

Then John Calipari visited.

He was at the University of Massachusetts, and he wasn't the huge coaching star he is today. But he was in the process of making UMass a national name, and there was no question he was a coach on the rise. There was starting to be a lot of excitement in Fall River about UMass, and Bobby Dempsey, the Durfee assistant coach, had once played there with both Julius Erving and Pitino. It was less than two hours away, it was the state university, and a lot of local people were pulling for me to go there.

But Calipari had gotten off to a bad start in this little recruiting battle, as he had told Mr. Karam that maybe I could go to prep school for a year because he didn't have enough scholarships left. Mr. Karam thought that was bullshit, that if Calipari really wanted me he'd find a scholarship. UMass also seemed to play a patterned offense that was about always trying to get the ball inside to the big men, and my father wasn't thrilled with that, as my game was better in the open court, better in transition. So that visit didn't go as well as the others. I never thought Calipari really wanted me; I had the sense that he was recruiting me because he thought he had to.

But that's the other thing about recruiting.

Sometimes it's more difficult for a local kid. They get scrutinized too much. There's too much familiarity.

Whatever the reason, after Calipari left that night I knew I wasn't going to UMass.

The last coach to visit was Jim O'Brien of Boston College. He came in the house carrying a carton of ice cream, like he was visiting a friend's house. He was. My mother loved him, thought he had been very good with Michael, even though Michael had left BC after a year and a half when he got hurt. But we had known O'Brien for five years or so, and he was one of those people everyone liked. I had met him years earlier, knew his daughters, and being recruited by him was like being recruited by your uncle. I had even been to his wife's funeral several years earlier. It was personal with us.

At one point my father voiced concern that Boston College might be too close to Fall River, just an hour away. His fear was that my friends would always be coming around. That was certainly a legitimate fear, but when I heard it I flipped out; my father and I verbally got into it a little bit, and I got all upset and stormed out of the house.

So the recruiting visit became O'Brien and my parents.

Then about a half hour later Michael walked in the house.

"How's the visit going?" he asked them as he came into the living room.

I made three campus visits that fall.

The first was to Syracuse.

Bernie Fine, the longtime assistant coach, was in charge of my visit, and he was great.

That night I was hanging out with Conrad McRae, Red Autry, and Luke Jackson, a few of the players, and we were at a bar on a street right next to the campus. All of a sudden a fight broke out between the football guys and the basketball guys over someone messin' with someone's girlfriend, and it spilled out to the campus across the street. Somehow I ended up in the middle of it, and I got clocked by a sucker punch. So by the time I met Boeheim in his office on Sunday, I had a black eye.

Again, Boeheim was very low-key.

He talked about how their up-tempo style of play was ideal for me.

He talked about their support system for athletes.

He said everything I wanted to hear.

"We think this is a great fit for you, Chris," he said.

He didn't even mention the black eye, as if some recruit having one was all part of the game.

I liked Syracuse. I liked Boeheim. I liked Bernie Fine. I liked Wayne Morgan, the other assistant. When I left I could see myself going there. It seemed to be the best of all worlds. It wasn't home, but Syracuse played every year in Boston, in Providence, and in Storrs, Connecticut, three places close enough so that my friends in Fall River could see me play. It was the Big East, it was the Carrier Dome with thirty thousand people, and they always seemed to be on national television. It had everything.

I was sure I was going to Syracuse.

Then I went to Wisconsin to visit. Stu Jackson, who is now one of the vice presidents of the NBA, was the coach. Stan Van Gundy, now the coach of the Orlando Magic, was the assistant, the one who had come to Durfee to recruit me. The school was beautiful, and they did the whole thing, introducing you out in the middle of the darkened arena, your name on a uniform. They treated you like you were already there, part of the family.

On the Saturday afternoon I visited we went to the Wisconsin football game at Camp Randall Stadium. That was the day a section of bleachers collapsed as kids were trying to rush the field after upsetting Michigan and seventy-three students were injured, six critically.

I felt like a black cat.

My last visit was to Florida. It was so big and overwhelming, I knew I wasn't going there, even though I felt bad about that because of Ron Stewart. I didn't want to tell him I wasn't coming.

There was a press conference at the Talbot Middle School in Fall River in October of my senior year. We had chosen it because it was the home of the Milliken League, and my brother and Leo arranged it. I hadn't wanted to do it, because I didn't think I could handle it. There were a few hundred people in the gym and what seemed like a dozen TV cameras. Mr. Karam was also there.

"This is a little different than in 1953 when I announced I was going to prep school," he said.

I was terrified, just wanted it to be over. It was completely nerve-wracking. I was totally sick of the whole recruiting thing, had come to see it as very destructive, not only for me, but for all the coaches who had spent so much time recruiting me, and now it was all for nothing. No one was supposed to know where I was going, but that day the *Boston Globe* stated that I was going to Syracuse.

As I stepped to the microphone, Eggie McRae, one of my BABC teammates, gave me a maroon and white Boston College cap. I put it on and turned to face the cameras.

"My brother went to Boston College, and I feel very comfortable with Coach O'Brien and have a good relationship with him," I said into the microphone.

It was the University of Fall River after all.

That's what it had come down to.

I had settled for the familiar, the comfortable. And maybe, deep down somewhere, I had chosen the place closest to home, so if I failed I wouldn't have that far to go.

There was still a senior year to play, of course, and much of it was a blur. I don't remember when I scored my two-thousandth point, or whom it came against. I don't remember when I became the all-time Durfee scoring leader. I don't even remember who beat us in the state tournament. It might have been Catholic Memorial in Boston, but maybe not. Your senior year is supposed to be so memorable, but to me it was something to get through before everything else started. I was back playing Somerset and Dartmouth, back hanging out in Suneson's house on weekends, back to life in Fall River. If anything, there was even more pressure to win the state championship because of the success I'd had over the summer and all the attention, but at some level it was as if it was all played out, too, as if I had outgrown it.

The spotlight was bigger, no question about it, and that caused trouble.

We got beat in the finals of a Christmas tournament in nearby Newport, Rhode Island, by a team from Bridgeport, Connecticut. Moments afterward, I went into the locker room and threw the all-tournament team trophy into a trash can. Second place wasn't enough in my house. You didn't bring those kinds of trophies home. It was reported in the *Newport Daily News,* though, and it became a big deal. Years later, if I ran into someone from Newport they still remembered it, the punk kid from Fall River who threw the trophy in the trash can.

There was a scuffle with some kids from Silver Lake after a high school hockey game in Fall River. It got me suspended from school for five days and was all over the Fall River *Herald News.* Then when I came back I was caught leaving school a half hour early with another kid. I got suspended again, missed a game, and, that, too, was on the front page of the paper. At one point my name was in the paper for over a week and none of it was for anything good.

Why was I being picked on?

They didn't have headlines in the paper about all the other kids who got caught leaving school early. Why was I the only one that was under a microscope? That was my mind-set back then, and nothing could change it. I couldn't understand that once I was news, I was news, good *and* bad. I couldn't understand why I wasn't treated like the other kids, because lots of kids got suspended from school and no one even knew about it.

Mr. Karam was always all over me—Chrissie this, Chrissie that, Chrissie, what are you doing?

"You've got the world in the palm of your hand and you're doing everything in your power to blow it," he said one day.

In retrospect, Mr. Karam was in a delicate situation. He had said I was the best player in Durfee history. I had been through a national recruiting process. I was averaging twenty-seven points a game. The word was I was going to be a McDonald's All-American. And here I was constantly in trouble, one little thing after another.

What was he supposed to do, throw me off the team?

But none of this registered. I was so caught up in the present tense, with what was right in front of my face. Around Christmas I wanted to leave, go finish the year at some prep school someplace, because it was like everything was closing in on me.

The negative publicity. The added pressure that came with being a big-time recruit. Being called the best player to ever come out of Fall River. It was like swimming around in a big fishbowl with everyone looking at me, and it simply reinforced to me how much I didn't like playing for Durfee, how nerve-wracking it was for me, how ambivalent I was about playing basketball in the first place. Because I never worked at it back then. I never lifted weights. I'd been smoking since I was twelve years old. I did dip. I didn't eat healthy. I never worked out on my own, never ran, and drank my brains out every weekend. It was like I was doing everything in my power not to be good.

Or maybe it was like this: If you had a job during the day that you didn't like, would you go home at night and work at it?

Probably not.

And that's what Durfee had become for me—a job I didn't like.

The games were like little pressure cookers. Not to mention little family dramas. My mother would sit on one side of the gym, and my father on the other. They would never sit together. If the game was going badly, my father would leave. If we lost and my brother was home from college—he went to Belmont Abbey in North Carolina—he'd be in the locker room afterward, telling us that we had no heart, that we weren't serious enough, that we were a disgrace to the city, that he and his teammates knew what it took to win a state championship and we didn't. That we drank too much, and smoked too much, and that even though he and his team certainly had done their share of partying, they had known when to get serious and take care of business, but we weren't doing that. Everything was the state championship. If you didn't win, you had failed. No in-between. It was that simple.

And if you didn't win, you didn't want Michael around.

It was that simple, too.

But then the actual game would start, and it was like someone flipped a switch. Off I went, the beast inside me coming out of his cage. Whether it was the adrenaline, the crowd, a fear of failure, whatever, I would want to take some kid's head off. Some nights, in parts of the game, the parts I played my best, I'd be off in what felt like some other dimension, someplace where everything seemed to be magnified. In those times I thought I could do anything. And if we lost, I was inconsolable, lacking the emotional skills to deal with losing or any kind of failure.

I wanted to run away and hide, be anywhere but where I was.

Mr. Karam and I seemed to circle around each other, waiting for the other shoe to drop.

Now, looking back, I can see that this was supposed to be his last great team, one last chance to win another state championship. He was thinking of stepping down as coach, and he wanted to go out with one more title, go out on top.

The team was good that year, but not great, probably the least talented team I had been on. It often seemed like it was me and Jeff Caron against the world. We didn't have enough size. We weren't good enough to win a state tournament, but in my mind it was like I had failed. My brother and his friends had won two state titles and my friends and I couldn't win one, and in Fall River that was all that mattered. There was no second place.

When the season ended I felt relief, like some giant weight had been lifted.

Then I had to go to New York and another miserable experience playing in the McDonald's All-American game. Don't misunderstand. Being named to the team was great, a tremendous honor for the school and for Fall River. On one level I certainly understood that. But back then McDonald's for me was not the high school all-star game, but the place we met in the shopping center near Durfee before we went out and got fucked up on a weekend night.

That was the reality of it.

That's what McDonald's meant to me.

Playing in the game was awful.

We were in New York for four or five days, and that was cool. The big name was Felipe López, the New York City kid who had already been profiled in *The New Yorker* and was being called the first Hispanic basketball superstar, the next Michael Jordan. We hung around a little bit. Antoine Walker was there. Raef LaFrentz. We worked out, visited a children's hospital, and all that was great.

Then there was the game. It was played at St. John's, and it was on national television. A bus full of people from Fall River made the four-hour trip.

I never got the ball.

On my team was a little guard from New York named Kareem Reid, who belonged in midget wrestling. He always had the ball, and it didn't take me long to realize that he was never going to pass it to me, that I was just part of his act, just a prop for what he thought was going to be his show.

I was distraught afterward. Felt humiliated, embarrassed. The game had been on national television and it had been a disaster. Or so I thought. I didn't want to show my face, as if I had failed in the most public of ways. I didn't want to go out and see the people from home who had made the bus trip. I was supposed to go to the Capital Classic in Washington, but I didn't want to go. I wanted to go someplace by myself and hide.

But my father came and put his arm around me. It was not the way he usually dealt with me after a bad game.

"You and I are going to go to Washington together," he said, "and it's going to be all right."

So we did.

And it was.

I had eighteen points in the game.

My father had been nurturing and reassuring and it had worked.

And the kicker to the McDonald's game?

A few weeks later I went up against Kareem Reid in an AAU tournament in Providence.

"I'm going to fuck you up," I said to him.

So every time I got the ball I went right at him, made him pay for the McDonald's game. Over and over I went right at him, and I kicked his ass.

This is what I knew. This is how I had grown up. This was the lesson I took with me out of my house. This was the lesson I learned in Fall River.

Be a wolf.

■CHAPTER FIVE■

The seniors at Boston College used to play Wiffle ball and drink beer in what was called "the Mods," a cluster of modern-looking town-house dorms across from Alumni Stadium. But they were going to graduate that year, and I was a freshman with no clue.

I had gone to Boston College with the best of intentions, as naïve as I was. I was ready to leave Fall River, and this was the next step. It was away from home, but not too far. I felt extremely comfortable with Jim O'Brien. I was comfortable in Boston. I was looking forward to college basketball.

The only problem?

It was college.

And I was in no way prepared to go to college. I didn't have any study habits. I didn't have any structure. I didn't have any discipline to even get up in the morning, never mind be a college student. I'd been sliding through school since the beginning, and now I was in a real school and woefully ill-prepared to be there.

I thought that's what college was, drinking beer and playing Wiffle ball. There was a big drinking and party culture at BC and I didn't know how to say no. There was always someone either drinking or planning to go out drinking; there was always a party someplace. And if it wasn't on campus, it was at the bars you could walk to. Never mind taking the T into Boston. It was all like one big neon sign.

I hardly ever went to class because I couldn't sit there. It was like torture. I don't think I attended even ten classes the whole time I was at Boston College. After a couple of weeks I had moved out of the freshman dorm and was staying in the rooms of some of the older players who lived in the Mods. I knew Bevan Thomas, one of the upperclassmen players, from BABC, and many nights I just slept on his floor. Eventually, O'Brien got wind of it and called me into his office. We genuinely liked each other; it wasn't just player and coach. I knew he was trying to help me, and not only because I was his prized recruit.

"What's the problem, Chris?" he asked. "Why aren't you living in your room?"

"What's the problem? I'm living in a ten-by-ten room with a six-foot-ten Canadian who has vampire posters on the wall. Who has Bruce Lee posters. That's the problem. You expect me to live in a room with vampire pictures on the wall?"

Then I wouldn't show up for study hall. It was mandatory for basketball players, four times a week. But I couldn't sit there for two hours. Besides, when I did go, there was nothing for me to do because I didn't go to class and didn't have any notes to study, or even know what books to read, which I wasn't going to read anyway, even if I'd had them.

Study hall?

Are you fuckin' kidding me?

A couple of the older players tried to help me, but there was no helping me. I was already beyond help. The rest of the guys were following the rules and I wasn't. It was as simple as that. I would look over at them in study hall and they'd be doing stuff. But I had nothing to do.

The rest of the students were from a different socioeconomic background. In my freshman dorm they would have pizza parties, movie parties—typical freshman stuff. I watched kids enjoy that. They thought it was fun. That wasn't me. I didn't think that was fun. I wanted to go out in Boston, go to clubs, get fucked up. I knew right from the beginning I didn't fit in, and I rebelled against that.

Sometime in the fall *Sports Illustrated* shot pictures of me jumping on a trampoline in front of Faneuil Hall in downtown Boston, near where the street vendors hung out. It was part of a big feature on incoming freshmen in the Big East—Felipe López of St. John's, Ray Allen of Connecticut, me. It was a big picture, complete with me in my maroon Boston College uniform, national exposure. Everyone saw it, made a big deal about it, and I could live off my laurels for a while longer. But I already knew I was in deep trouble.

Then I got hurt in my first game, falling on my left wrist in the second half and breaking it. It was a home game against Cal

Poly, and when I went down I knew it was serious. I had scored fourteen points by then, was having a good game, but after that I knew I was fucked. Basketball was the only chance of helping me get through Boston College, the only thing that gave me any focus at all. Without it? It was just a matter of time.

Then I found cocaine.

Or maybe it found me.

I had always been afraid of cocaine, had never seen it in Fall River. I was afraid of it because of Len Bias. I had been a kid when Len Bias died of a cocaine overdose two days after he got drafted by the Celtics in 1986; the same Len Bias who everyone said was going to be a great NBA player. Because of that I wanted no part of cocaine.

But there it was one night in a dorm room, on offer by a guy and girl.

"Do you want some?" the guy asked.

"No."

"Come on," he said. "Try it."

I hesitated.

"Just put it on your gums," the girl said.

I was off and running.

I never wanted to put cocaine down. Everyone else would be coming home at one, two in the morning, shutting it down, and I'd be making that one more call, knocking on someone's door, looking to keep it going. I couldn't stop. Did I know what I was doing? I didn't care. I would go to bed with my heart racing. Eventually, it would slow down and I'd fall asleep. Over St. Patrick's Day that year I went to South Boston to see the parade and I saw the clock go around twice. I got back to my dorm and lay on the floor, my heart beating so fast my shirt was going up and down. I thought I was going to die.

But it was all about keeping the party going.

Cocaine extended the night. I never did it without drinking first, but eight or nine beers didn't do it for me. I'd be swaying back and forth. I wasn't a good drunk. I wasn't content with that. I needed more of a bite, more bark. Cocaine is a very revealing drug. There was no filter, at least not for me. I'd end up telling some stupid girl that I used to wet the bed as a kid. Crazy shit. You end up talking about the most intimate things in a room full of strangers. You never knew what was going to happen with cocaine, but for me it all started with alcohol.

O'Brien was always bringing me into his office. They used to drug test us sporadically at Boston College, and I had already failed two for marijuana. If you failed three you were ineligible for an entire year, so of course he was very concerned with that. He was also very concerned with my schoolwork, or lack of it. So one day he brought me into the office of Chet Gladchuk, the Boston College athletic director. He was one of those no-nonsense guys who looked like he should have been in the military. His kid was also a freshman, walking around the campus in polo shirts with the collar up, all prepped out, and I had already had two run-ins with him, had already threatened him twice. So me and Gladchuk didn't have a whole lot of good karma going on between us.

"We're going to try to help you," Gladchuk said, taking out a pad and putting it in front of him. "Tell me the names of your classes and your teachers."

I couldn't do it.

The only thing I knew was that one of my teachers was a nun.

"What's her name?" Gladchuk asked.

The silence hung in the room.

"I don't know," I finally said. "Sister Something."

That was it.

Or at least close to it.

The end came the day O'Brien's secretary called and said that he was going to call me in the basketball office. He was at the Final Four. It was late March.

By this time O'Brien was understandably tired of me. He had done everything he could, and nothing had worked. I wasn't hearing it. I was out all night in Boston clubs. I had been at BC for seven months but I knew more about Mary Ann's, the bar near campus, and Copperfield's, near Fenway Park, than I did about Boston College. I had crossed worlds. I wasn't hanging with students anymore. I was with people in Kenmore Square, people all over the city, and cocaine was everywhere. I never had to pay for it. And if it was around, I was going to use. That's just the way it was, the way it had become. I knew it was all fucked up, but this was my life, going out at night and sleeping all day, as if I was powerless to stop it. I had stopped going to class a long time ago. I couldn't play basketball. I was a total delinquent, and I knew the gig was up.

"Chris, you're doing cocaine now?" O'Brien said over the phone.

There was real concern in his voice, but this had been my third failed drug test. It was over.

"I've already called your parents," he said.

I walked out of the office in tears.

I arrived at a tiny airport in Fresno, California, in the summer of 1995.

It was a short trip from San Francisco in a little airplane, and the airport was in the middle of nowhere, surrounded by farmland. I felt like it was on the moon.

It was about fifteen minutes to the Fresno State campus, and that was another shock. It was full of square, functional buildings, most of them white, and none of them big. It looked like a community college, with parking lots everywhere. It was nothing like I envisioned a major college to be. In the middle of the campus was the agriculture department, complete with animals walking around. What the fuck was this? It was a long way from Boston College. Nor was it Wisconsin, or Syracuse, or the University of Florida. The only gym on campus was a small practice gym. It looked like an old CYO gym. I had been picked up at the airport by Danny Tarkanian, who had played for his father at UNLV, and John Welch. They were the two assistants.

That first night I was driven to a condo near the campus and given a key. There was no furniture. No electricity. I ended up at a pay phone in the parking lot of a Jack in the Box talking to Heather. We probably talked for two hours, me saying I couldn't do this, and her talking me down.

That was what she always did for me. That was the connection we had, the bond we had. We would go along for a while in our own worlds, she with other boyfriends, me with other girlfriends, but at all the important times, she was the one I'd call. Heather was always there, always loyal, never judged me. She was more important than my girlfriends, and I was more important than her boyfriends. That was the relationship we had had since the sixth grade, and in that spring of 1995, when everything was falling apart, we had it.

I didn't meet Jerry Tarkanian until a couple of days later, but he was the reason I was there.

Because in my mind I didn't have any other place to go.

My world had imploded shortly after I had left O'Brien's office. A story ran in the *Boston Globe* by Will McDonough, one of the media stars in Boston. He had been there forever and also worked for CBS as a sideline reporter on NFL games, and he was very friendly with both Red Auerbach and Bill Parcells. He was a heavyweight, a Boston institution. He was known for having the inside scoop, and he certainly had it that day. It was all there: the failed drug tests, the cocaine, the missed classes, the expulsion. Boston College wasn't going to let me go softly, and, in retrospect, they had every right not to. They had invested in me, and it had blown up in their face. But McDonough exposed me. If I had had any innocence left from my basketball journey, it went away that day.

My first reaction?

I wanted his address, because I wanted to go there and punch him out.

Most of all, though, I wanted to dig a hole in the dirt and just hide. I wanted to go back to Fall River and disappear in someone's basement and not show my face. My gig was up in the worst possible way. My friends were still trying to sneak by their parents using breath mints and squirting cologne on their clothes to hide the smell like we used to do in high school, and I was all over the *Boston Globe* for using cocaine.

This wasn't drinking in Suneson's basement. It wasn't running from the cops in the woods at a keg party in Fall River. It wasn't even doing coke at BC on the sly, even if people on campus knew about it. This was all my problems laid out for the world to see. It would have been embarrassing enough to have been thrown out of Boston College, never mind the substance abuse. I wanted to run away and never come back.

I had a raging cocaine problem, my parents were living in separate houses and talking about getting divorced, and I had no idea what I was going to do.

Then I got a call from Jerry Tarkanian.

I didn't even know Tark was still coaching; I thought he'd retired. And I had been a Duke fan as a kid, and Tark and the "Runnin' Rebels" of UNLV had been the enemy. At the time

I didn't know that Tark had played at Fresno State in the mid 1950s, or that he had begun his coaching career at a high school in Fresno. I didn't know that he'd coached at a junior college in California before getting the Long Beach State job in the late 1960s. There, he was one of the first coaches in Division I to recruit a lot of junior college players, and he turned Long Beach State into a regional power, bringing them from nowhere. I didn't know that he had coached for twenty years at UNLV, where he went to four Final Fours and won the national title in 1991, beating Duke by thirty to do so. I didn't know any of that when I first got to Fresno.

But I knew he was called "Tark the Shark." I knew who he was, that's for sure. I knew some of his guys had been caught in a hot tub with a gambler. I knew he was the guy always chewing on the white towel, the guy who had coached the Runnin' Rebels, the guy who had been in the basketball movie *Blue Chips*. I knew he was the star of Gucci Row in Vegas, the unofficial name for all the money guys with the gold chains who sat courtside.

He said he was coaching at Fresno State.

I didn't know where Fresno was.

"I'm starting over, Chris," he said on the phone. "I'm going back to my hometown, my alma mater, to do it all over again."

He also said I was a kid who was broken down, someone who needed another chance, and maybe we could do it together.

"I'm in," I told him. He had me, hook, line, and sinker.

He didn't have to say another word.

He was in his office the first time I met him. It was tiny,

something like twelve-by-twelve, and it had pictures of bull-dogs on the walls. The Fresno Bulldogs.

But there was no glamour necessary.

Tark was the glamour, with his red Adidas sweat suits and his big national championship ring on his finger.

He was a cross between the greatest salesman in the world and your grandfather. He had a shaved head and hangdog eyes and this incredibly kind face, and he looked at you like he had seen it all and nothing was going to surprise him. It was very comforting. In all the time I was there, I never felt like a product. Tark was the best of the best. We had a different relationship. We were together a lot, and he always made me feel like his kid. By the time I got to him, Coach Tark had already made his reputation coaching a whole shitload of so-called troubled kids. Larry Johnson. Stacey Augmon. That nutcase from New York, Lloyd Daniels. The players who had gotten photographed in a hot tub in Vegas with a guy who had been accused of fixing games, Richie "The Fixer" Perry. Tark was great with guys like that. Trust me, I wasn't the first dysfunctional kid he ever coached.

And the message?

Hard work.

He let me know that if I did what he asked, I could get it all back.

He let me know that I could put the past behind me and have a second act.

He let me know that if I worked hard, all my basketball dreams could still come true, that they didn't have to end in shame and regret.

How could you not like that?

Coach Tark was amazing. Here he was in his seventies, but he was still getting after it. He was us in an old man's body. That was his gift.

No matter how much money he made, or how many games he won, his feet never left the ground. He never changed. That skinny guy who played JJ on the TV show *Good Times* would come in. Or James Caan, the actor, would come in. And Tark would never change, not one bit.

One day I went into his office. It was my first summer at Fresno and I was homesick.

"Coach," I said, the anxiety in my voice, "I'm three thousand miles from home, I'm homesick, and I have no money."

He looked at me, and then said in that soft voice of his, "Chris, you have no money?"

"No, Coach. I'm three thousand miles from home, and I have no money."

He looked at me for a few seconds, didn't say anything, then put his hand in his pocket, took out seven rumpled dollars, and gave them to me.

"Here, Chris," he said. "Here's some money."

You weren't getting any money from Coach Tark.

You were getting a second chance.

■CHAPTER SIX■

Boston College had blown up, and this was a second chance.

This is what I told myself over and over. It was Coach Tark's message. I had been broken, but this was going to be my redemption.

That first summer I ended up living with Danny Tarkanian and John Welch. They lived in a town house near campus. It was a nice place with a pool. I had my own room. I was enrolled at Fresno City College, which was downtown, about fifteen minutes away, but I didn't go there often. Danny and Welch might have thought I was going to school all the time, but I had the sense that academics would be taken care of, that everyone was on the same page. My real life was in the gym. I was a prisoner of John Welch. He had been a guard at UNLV, and he set out to get me back in shape. It was like a basketball boot camp. It was ninety degrees and we were in the gym day after day. I had arrived in terrible shape, probably thirty pounds overweight, because I really hadn't played since November. Thirty pounds overweight and with a drug problem to boot.

His message was simple: you got better in the gym.

If there were twenty-four hours in the day, he wanted you in there twenty-eight.

Danny Tarkanian had a lot of responsibility. He was his father's right hand, did a lot of the behind-the-scenes stuff, handled a lot of the academic stuff.

Danny was great with me. He went out of his way to help people. Did he get my problems? Did he understand them? No. But he had been a good point guard at UNLV for his father, and he had a great sense of the game. Danny and I were more friends than we were player-coach. We would go out together once in a while.

His message to me then?

Moderation.

I was the first recruit of this new era at Fresno State; the other players were holdovers from the old coaching staff and felt like stepkids. They were all black, and some were Crips and some were Bloods.

No joke.

They were all mostly from LA. The Bloods wore red, and the Crips wore blue. You would never see them without their colors. The Bloods and the Crips were fighting for supremacy. Their feud was big in hip-hop music. Wars in hip-hop had been started over it. Countless people had died because of it. Their colors were their nationality. California was thick with gang life, and this was what they had grown up with.

They coexisted on the team, they figured it out, but they always flashed their gang signs when they made a basket, the Bloods holding their index finger and thumb together like they were forming a *B*, and the Crips making a *C* with their fingers.

That was the team when I first got there—the Bloods, the Crips, a big German, and me. But I got along with all of them.

In a sense we were all the same, all starting over.

Fresno was like nothing I had ever seen before.

It's 200 miles north of Los Angeles, and 180 miles south of San Francisco, in California's Central Valley: farm country. There were fig trees, and the Sierra Nevada mountains on one side. It was about an hour from Yosemite National Park. Every day in the summer it seemed like it was in the nineties, and there was a lot of wet fog in the winter, more fog than you'd ever seen in your life. There was a sense of isolation, like you were in the middle of nowhere, especially for someone like me who was coming from New England, where everything seems so closed in. The downtown was old and cramped, and we rarely went there except to play the games. The action was in the theater district. It was artsy, and that's where a lot of the nightclubs and bars were. It was about fifteen minutes from where I was living, but then everything in Fresno was fifteen minutes away.

A lot of the power brokers in the city were of Armenian heritage, and I learned that the Armenians had gone through one of the worst genocides in history, in 1915. They were great people, earthy, no pretense, reminded me of the people in Fall River. They were loyal to a fault. If you were one of theirs, they couldn't do enough for you, and they were totally committed to Fresno basketball. Tark was one of theirs, and his coming back to Fresno State was huge. Not only was it national news and meant some nationally televised games in the future, but it was going to put Fresno on the map. It was going to put Fresno State, long thought of as one of the stepchildren of the California state university system, on the map, too. The same Fresno State that schools like Stanford, UCLA, USC, and Berkeley would always look down on was going to be one of the new powers of college basketball, was going to do what UNLV had done in the 1970s.

That was the promise, anyway, and the entire city was into it. You could smell it in the air.

Tark's place was the Elbow Room in old Fresno. It was a dingy dive on one side, with a great restaurant on the other. The Elbow Room had a certain dark side to it; you had the sense that you could probably find anything there. There was a lot of action in Fresno. Every once in a while Tark would invite the team out to dinner, maybe fifteen of us.

"Order what you want," he'd say.

So we'd all order what we wanted, and the food would come, and it would be great, and afterward you'd look around and Tark would be gone and there'd be a bill for something like $600.

Tark never paid.

He was the man.

The word was he had never paid in Vegas, and he wasn't paying here, either.

That was part of the deal.

Tark was all business. He wasn't a screamer. The only time he did scream was when he had run out of everything else, and thought that screaming at us might get our attention. But that really wasn't his style. Going to practice was like going to work. You were expected to work hard, perform. And it was simple with him. You were either contributing or you weren't playing. There was a lot at stake, and this was serious.

Of all the coaches I ended up playing for, Tark was the toughest, made you work the hardest. We'd have preseason workouts and he'd have us in a defensive stance for forty-five minutes at a time. Try and do that for five minutes, never mind forty-five. And some of this would be happening at five thirty in the morning to beat the heat, because in the afternoon it might get up to 110 degrees.

But Tark and I had a special relationship. He kind of softened when he was with me. We would talk about our families. He liked hearing about Fall River; he was intrigued by it. He had read *Fall River Dreams,* and when people came out from Fall River, he would ask them about the city. I also think he was intrigued by me, by the fact that I was as good as I was and I was white, because there weren't a lot of us around. He was always saying I was the next Jerry West, which I never took seriously for a minute. To me, Jerry West was a smooth guy in a sport jacket.

Then again, Tark was the greatest salesman in the world.

And I certainly wasn't behaving like Jerry West, although back then I was the only one who knew that.

But I'm getting a little ahead of myself here.

In the beginning I knew I had to make the most of the opportunity in Fresno, and I had two friends in Danny and Coach Welch. Once in a while I'd go out drinking with Danny, because he figured I was a college kid and that's what college kids did, and he knew I was three thousand miles away from home and didn't have any friends yet. But he was concerned about me. Welch didn't drink, and he would sometimes drop me off at twelve-step meetings.

But my life was in the gym that summer. Working out three times a day. Riding the bike. Lifting. Eating healthy. All the shit I had never done before. Coach Welch changed my addiction into a workout addiction. I was his project, and he was a great teacher. I was extremely focused in the gym, and I was still under the radar. But I was in great shape for the first time in my life, and no one in the gym could guard me. And there was great competition. Guys were always coming through Fresno, and we'd have intense pickup games. Bruce Bowen and Ike Austin, two NBA guys who were from Fresno. DeShawn Stevenson, a high school kid in Fresno who would bypass college and go straight to the NBA. Lamar Odom, who was out there one time on a recruiting visit. I had picked him up at LAX in a rental car and we got into an accident before we even left the parking lot, but we had some good times, Lamar and I. Jason Kidd was there for a few days one summer, because one of his high school friends was Kris Stone, the Fresno team manager. Plus, we had the guys who weren't eligible playing, or the guys who had transferred in and were going to sit out the next year. They were all there playing in these pickup games, because in the summer no one was ineligible.

If you didn't get better in Fresno it was your own fault.

When I did go out drinking I didn't drink to be social. I drank to get wasted. That was the problem, but I don't think people saw it as a big deal then, since I was a nineteen-year-old college kid and some of that was expected. The first year there I didn't do it very often. For the most part my addiction was under control. The few times I did cocaine it was very hush-hush. Afterward, I felt two feet tall and would go back to the gym the next day and work out twice as hard.

My entire first year I was only involved in one incident, but even that drew a lot of publicity. Everything we did in Fresno got a lot of publicity. We were like the Patriots in Boston, on TV seven days a week. You'd come out of practice and there would be cameras in your face. The *Fresno Bee* had three reporters covering us, and two of them—Adrian Wojnarowski and Andy Katz—turned covering Fresno State basketball into big-time jobs. Katz now covers college basketball for ESPN, and Wojnarowski covers the NBA for Yahoo! Sports. The Fresno fans were incredibly passionate, and we were treated like their pro team.

I was with Danny and a few other teammates. We were at a restaurant a few miles from campus called the Black Angus. I got into an argument with a wrestler, a bouncer got involved, and before I knew what was happening, it had spilled out into the parking lot and a SWAT team had shown up. It was all over the media, going out on the national wire because it was Jerry Tarkanian and Fresno State, but it quickly blew over.

Under NCAA rules I had to sit out that year because I was technically a transfer, even though Boston College had thrown me out, so there was no pressure. I didn't go to school much, but it wasn't like it was Harvard. I was always in the gym, in the best shape of my life. I had been such a mess when I first arrived, but now I'd lost the weight and my quickness was back. Never again would I be in the shape I was in that year. I was living in the house of a booster named Mike and his wife, Andie. They had three young kids, two boys and a girl, and I had my own room. They were a family and I was a part of it. It was all part of the strategy to keep me on the straight and narrow, keep me contained. For the most part it worked that year. I would fall off the planet once in a while, but only once in a while, and I was still beneath the radar.

That changed the next year.

Changed big-time.

There were only two white kids on the team, me and the big kid from Germany, but that didn't matter to me. That was basketball. If I had been at a place with a lot of white players it would have been Princeton, right? The brothers were there, and I was there, and that was it. I'd be at parties where I was the only white person. In turn, I'd take the black players to keg parties at fraternities, places they hadn't been before. But there were people in Fresno that would give me shit about it. I was in a liquor store once when these two bruisers came up to me.

"Why do you spend so much time with niggers?" one guy asked.

"What did you just say?" I asked.

We were about to get into it when a black guy named Carl Ray Harris, who had been a big star at Fresno a decade earlier, got involved. He was a Fresno legend, tough and street-smart, and he knocked out both of those big country boys.

But it was already starting to slide for me. My teammates would go out, smoke a few blunts, and drink some malt liquor. Then they'd go home. Their night was ending and mine was just beginning. I was living in two different worlds. Danny and Coach Welch knew. They were always talking to me about the future, about how far I could go if I just kept working and stayed home at night. They got on me about going out and the choices I made once I got there. But that didn't matter to me. I didn't care about the future.

Career?

I'd go out drinking to think about it.

I was a walking contradiction that year. I'd go out and get fucked up, coming in to Mike and Andie's house in the early morning when the birds were chirpin' and the kids were getting ready to go off to school. I'd put curtains on the wall to block out the sun, to try to get my heart to stop racing so I could sleep. Then when I woke up I'd feel so guilty I'd go to the gym and take five hundred jumpers.

It was never about the future for me. It was about today. People ask me now why someone didn't stop me. It's the wrong question.

No one *could* stop me.

When the next season started, so did life in the fishbowl. Our first road game was at Oregon, and they started on me before the game began. Guys were in the student section screaming "Fall River Nightmare" at me, over and over. I was in the middle of the storm, just like I had been in high school, and I really didn't know why. Why were they messin' with me? Were they really talking to me like this? I couldn't understand it.

Then they started charting my warm-up shots, yelling after every shot, and the more I missed, the more they yelled. At one point I was something like three for thirty, and they're yelling, and the more they yell, the more I miss.

After that I was done for the game.

Done.

The game starts and Oregon has this six-foot-six brother who is draped all over me. Forget "Fall River Nightmare." The game was a nightmare. We were awful, and I was praying for it to end. It was a total fuckin' disaster.

And the "Fall River Nightmare" stuff came straight from *Fall River Dreams*.

Fall River Dreams had come out in the fall of 1994, when I was at Boston College, and it was a problem.

In the beginning I was insecure about it, like I was being exposed.

Because it's about you. But it's about you the way you once were, like you're forever trapped in a moment of time, forever seventeen years old. I was always getting questions about it.

People asked me to sign it. I probably signed thousands of them. We'd go on road trips at Fresno and the boosters on the plane would all be reading it. Some people would say they felt sorry for me. Others wanted to meet me because of it. They wanted me to answer questions about it. In every article that was ever written about me the book was mentioned. "Chris Herren, who is in the book *Fall River Dreams*."

Jeff Caron, who played college ball at Merrimack, said that he knew kids who had some of the dialogue memorized.

I got it all, from "You're a fuckin' punk" to "Can I have your autograph?"

To this day I sometimes get defensive about it.

There was never any running away from it.

The "Fall River Nightmare" in that first game told me that.

But if my reception at Oregon was bad, the one at the University of Massachusetts was ten times worse. UMass is in the western part of the state, about two hours from Fall River, and it was my unofficial homecoming. There were scores of people there for me, and UMass was nationally ranked. They had a backcourt of Edgar Padilla and Carmelo Travieso, with whom I had played at BABC, so it couldn't have been any more emotionally loaded for me.

Oh yeah, it was also on ESPN.

About an hour before the game I went out into the Mullins Center to shoot, and already there were a ton of kids behind the basket where I was shooting.

"Druggie . . . druggie . . . druggie," they chanted.

"You suck, Herren!" they yelled.

"Cocaine . . . cocaine."

"Fall River Nightmare."

"Herren sucks."

I was probably out there for about fifteen minutes, and it never stopped.

Welcome home.

I had a huge game that night, twenty-five points, and that elevated me nationally. After that I was a star, at least in Fresno.

I was white and I played with passion. That's what drove it. They started selling my jersey in the school store. A Japanese restaurant about two miles from school put me on the menu, number 24, chicken and rice with salad on top. I ate there every day, and Ted Kunishige never let me pay. I'd go into the kitchen and make my own dish.

We played downtown in a place called Selland Arena. It sat about ten thousand people, and it was about five miles from the school. It was old and funky, complete bedlam. We never practiced there, but we loved playing there. We would come out of the tunnel and run through two rows of fans, and it was sheer lunacy. It was like the energy picked you up and put you on the floor, and there were nights when I'd be in the zone, the way I'd sometimes been in high school. When I was in that state it was like everything was magnified. I was so tuned in it was like looking at a TV screen in high definition before there was high definition. I knew where everyone was sitting. It was like I could hear their conversations, and I wanted to join in. It had happened to me several nights in high school; this feeling would just come over me out of nowhere, and I felt like I could do anything, like it was my ball and my game and the other players were just props.

Sometimes the game would slow down, and sometimes it would speed up and go too fast, and I wanted to slow it down and stay in that state forever.

That was the year everything changed. I went from being under the radar to being right in the middle of the radar. Everyone wanted to get to know me, everyone from CEOs, to kids with eight balls of coke in their pockets, to gangbangers. I never paid for anything in restaurants. I never paid for anything anywhere. It was like being on scholarship everywhere I went. I got invited to kids' birthday parties. I got fan mail all the time. I still get letters and notes from people in Fresno. People send me pictures they want autographed. The people in Fresno couldn't have been any better to me. They were very forgiving. I ran amok and they still loved me. But I was visible in the community, too. I spoke at schools. I ran a youth league in the Hmong community that began as a summer project I did for a class. I loved both those things. I'd always loved kids, being around them, coaching them. It made me feel good, gave me the sense that for all my issues, there was still a part of me that hadn't been corrupted yet, something that was still pure.

I loved Fresno.

But the more I went out, the more ugly things were starting to get.

I was already living in the basketball world and the drug world. I knew the lingo of drugs. I knew how to get them, knew all the signs. The guy who makes too many trips to the bathroom. The guy who says he wants to party with you. All too soon I knew who had it and who sold it.

San Francisco was only two and a half hours away, and every once in a while another guy and I would go up to the big rave clubs there, where the drug of choice was Ecstasy. It's a gross drug, because you never slow down. You end up sweating bullets like you just played in five NBA games. You're high for hours at a time, because you keep doing it over and over.

How many will you take?

As many as you can get your hands on.

By this time I had two tattoos and this fueled my notoriety, too. I got the first one, HERREN and my family crest high on my right arm, in Fresno, when I was drunk. The second came at Venice Beach in LA, a small shamrock on my left forearm. I was drunk then, too.

Would I have gotten them if I hadn't been drunk?

Probably.

Why did I get them?

The simple reason was Damon Stoudamire had his name on his arm and I liked that.

The more complicated reason?

I liked doing things that were different, that pushed buttons. Whatever the reasons, I was the perfect victim for a tattoo artist. I was also the perfect victim for a hairstylist. First it was streaks in my dark hair. Then for a while my hair was platinum. That was just another button to push. Once I started getting in trouble I wasn't looking for approval or disapproval. In retrospect, the hair and the tattoos were minor. But once you're labeled it's like your head is on a swivel. You become wary of people after you get in trouble. You don't trust them. You think they all want something from you. But I became my own worst enemy, too, because I used my notoriety. Free drinks. Free drugs. Free entrée into any world I wanted to go into.

Not that the team didn't have its own notoriety.

Sports Illustrated called us "Last Chance U," and just about all of us had started off somewhere else. Fresno was the last stop. Terrence Robinson, a three-time Parade All-American, had been kicked off his high school team in Michigan before the state tournament started. Daymond Forney, who was as talented as anyone I played with in Fresno, had been raised in a crack house, smoking pot since he was nine years old. He had been thrown out of two junior colleges. An assistant coach from the last coaching regime had told Tark that, in his opinion, Dominick Young would destroy his team. Rahsaan Smith, our six-foot-ten center, had been to two junior colleges and told *SI* that we were like the Bad News Bears. Everywhere we went it was like the circus was coming to town, with Tark as the ringleader, sitting on the bench and chewing on his white towel.

Still, the longer the season went on, the better I played, and the more attention I got.

NBA guys were always coming in and out of Fresno.

Danny Ainge. Rick Carlisle. Don Nelson. Jerry West. They all were great with me, talking with me, leaving periodic messages. West and I talked on the phone one time, and he was very positive, telling me I had a future in the game if I continued to stay strong and do the right thing. I felt almost giddy just talking to him.

I was putting up big numbers, getting a lot of publicity everywhere I went, and people were telling me the sky was the limit.

That was when the wannabe agents started coming out. They were called "runners" and they were always around, trying to get in with you, stuffing money in your pockets. They would tell you anything, give you anything. Some were real agents. Some worked for agents. Some were trying to be agents. But they all had the same agenda: to own a piece of you.

I knew it was getting out of control when my teammates would run away from me at night. They didn't want to go to my 'hood after midnight, because to do that would be to jump into my nightmare. Invariably, I'd end up partying with the Fresno Bulldogs, a Mexican gang that dressed in the team colors, red and white. They were no joke. They were gangbangers, guys with tattoos on their necks, on their heads. They've been on the History Channel, right there with the Hells Angels, the Latin Kings, and the Crips and the Bloods. A lot of them went to the games, were big fans, and I'd end up doing blow with them and their girlfriends. They'd look after me.

I'd get home at seven in the morning. That's when it would hit me the most. The whole world was getting ready to go out into the day, people leaving for work, little kids at the bus stop, and I'd be stumbling home after torturing myself all night, putting blankets over the windows to keep the light out, hating myself, the depression coming over me like the fog, wanting to run away and never come back. It was all beginning to feel like Boston College, everything spiraling out of control.

Never again, I'd tell myself.

Never ever ever again.

Then I'd sleep for a while and everything would look different. And by nighttime I'd have forgotten how bad it had been the night before, and I'd go out again, as if I could have stopped, even if I'd wanted to.

I would go to school every once in a while, just enough to stay eligible.

Tark would put an arm around me in practice.

"Chris, you've got to get your shit together," he would say. "You've got to go to class."

But Tark's life was all basketball. He delegated academics. There were people who took care of that, a big support system.

What was his great line at UNLV years earlier, when he had been presented with the fact that something like only 20 percent of his players ever graduated?

"Yeah," he said. "The guys that should have graduated did, and the ones that shouldn't didn't."

That was Tark. There was never any bullshit about him. He was giving you a chance, but you were expected to be adult enough to take care of yourself, smart enough to realize you were being given a second chance and to make the most of it. He had been around too long to hold your hand.

He only got involved when it was getting out of control. And when it did I would go to my teachers and ask to maybe do something for extra credit, apologize for not going to class all the time, beg, do anything to stay eligible. I was majoring in communications, and the teachers wanted to help you, wanted you to do well. But academics were never my focus. I always viewed school as one more opponent.

I was already on a personal descent, even though I had a great season. I was still in great shape despite all the crazed nights, was still able to get away with it. I had two years of college left, but I was already being mentioned as a definite NBA prospect. After the Western Athletic Conference tournament in Vegas, where I lit it up, agents were telling me to come out now for the NBA, sign with them, as they stuffed money in my pockets.

In a sense that was tempting, because Dominick Young was being accused of conspiring with some local gamblers to shave points in exchange for money.

Then I got implicated, too.

The stories broke in the *Fresno Bee*, fueled by the fact that both Dominick and I had been seen, at various times, in the company of guys known to be gamblers. No big surprise, at least in my case. When I was out and about, it often seemed like I was in the company of everyone. And there was a mall I often went to, and one of the stores was a jewelry store, and I would bullshit with the guy who owned it. He had a porn shop, too. He was in his mid-thirties and a big fan. We would talk about basketball, but everyone in Fresno talked about basketball. How are you guys going to do tonight? Can you beat Utah? What was I going to say? No? But is that giving information to gamblers? Telling them you think you're going to win in casual conversation? The newspaper stories tried to make it out like I was looking for friends in Fresno. I had enough friends. I didn't want to get to know you. It was in and out.

All that stuff got blown up into something it never was. There were so many rumors. People were saying my phone was tapped. I had reporters outside my apartment. There had always been cameras and sportswriters at practice. Now there was a whole other level of reporters every day.

Then one day I was called to the president's office and four FBI agents were there in their dark suits and narrow ties.

"We know you know things," one of them said.

"We want to help you," another one said.

I paused.

They kept pressing me.

"I want a lawyer," I said.

Why did I say that?

I knew it from TV, from movies. I knew I shouldn't be in a room with four FBI agents without someone looking out for my best interests.

I never heard from those four agents again.

But it was a national story, and every time it ran anywhere, my name was mentioned. It went on for years. Every Thursday the grand jury would meet in Fresno, and it would be all over the media. Just when it seemed like it was dying down, the grand jury would reconvene, and everything would start all over. And once again I was in the news for all the wrong reasons.

My world had changed.

It was no longer just about basketball.

There was no more innocence, if there ever had been. It was all business. Maybe I had first learned that at Boston College when they gave that story to Will McDonough in the *Boston Globe*. Good luck, kid. My view of college basketball had been tainted, and now I had agents handing me $100 bills on the sneak, and if they were trying to buy me, then they would have to pay more. That's how twisted I was.

It wasn't about basketball anymore.

Because when you get notoriety, all the creeps come out.

And one of them was me.

Our family in Fall River: Michael, me, my father, and my mother.

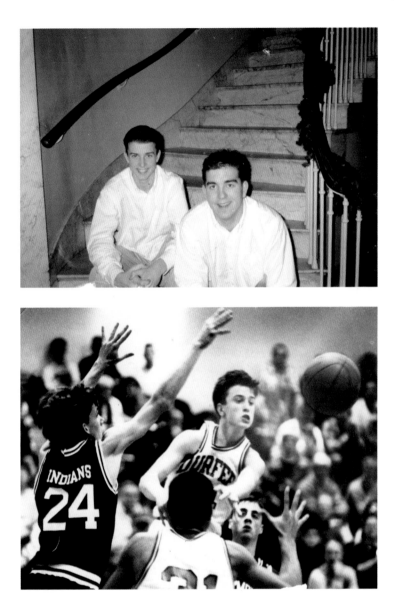

TOP: Michael and me at home. Growing up in a sports-crazy city, he was my mentor and protector.

BOTTOM: Driving the lane and passing the ball for Durfee High School. (*The Fall River Herald News*)

TOP: Me and Heather as high school sweethearts. I fell in love with her when we first met in sixth grade.

BOTTOM: Coach Jerry Tarkanian gave me a second chance at Fresno State.

OPPOSITE TOP: We played some unusual games at Fresno, including this one against Silute, a Lithuanian team. *(Mary Parker)*

OPPOSITE BOTTOM: The "Herren" tattoo, with family crest, and frosted hair was part of the circus at Fresno. *(Mary Parker)*

ABOVE: A second round pick by the Denver Nuggets, I learned that the NBA moves at a different speed: much faster, more powerful, and more competitive than you can imagine. *(Mary Parker)*

Playing for the Celtics was a New England kid's dream come true.
(The Boston Herald)

TOP: An off day in Beijing with our daughter, Samantha, trying to resurrect my basketball career in the Chinese Basketball Association.

BOTTOM: With our older son Christopher and Sammy at home.

Heather, me, Sammy, Chris, and newborn Drew.

■CHAPTER SEVEN■

It all went public in November 1997, my junior year, as public as a press conference on ESPN.

The announcement was that I was leaving the Fresno State basketball team and going to rehab, that I had "slipped up" in my fight against substance abuse.

The truth was I had already failed innumerable drug tests at Fresno. They were constantly testing me.

How many times?

Too many for my liking.

I was always in some kind of program. Everybody in the athletic department was aware of it. I went to an outpatient treatment center at Fresno called Cedar Vista. I went to counselors. I went to therapists. The people at Fresno State tried to help me, maybe too much. They hired people. One day a pastor knocked on the door and said he wanted to talk. Former players talked to me. One counselor was great. I saw him off and on for two and a half years.

In a sense they were the worst kind of enablers, even if they had good intentions. There's no question there were doctors and people who cared about me and were trying to deal with my addiction issues. Yet I had the sense that it was all about getting me ready to play, as if that's what we were there for.

It was only a couple of days after we had beaten UMass in Fresno. The game was on ESPN. I had been the star of the game, interviewed by ESPN afterward, even though I had spent the night before blasted on coke. I hadn't slept in what seemed like days, and two girls had dropped me at the arena shortly before the game. At first, I didn't think I could play, I was so fucked up, but the adrenaline kicked in and I went from there.

But I had never been so miserable. I just couldn't do it anymore. Seeing the sun come up. My mind racing out of control. The lies. The self-hatred. I knew I needed help, so I called Tark and told him I was struggling. The school was super. They essentially gave me two options. They would say that I had come down with the flu or some other ailment and would be back when I was ready, or they could say in a press release that I was taking some time off to deal with personal issues.

I decided to tell the truth.

For once, I wanted to stand up and take responsibility.

The press conference was right before Thanksgiving and my mother was there, as she and my grandfather had flown out for the UMass game.

"I've battled a personal problem for the past four years," I said through tears. "It's a winnable problem, but I've had a setback, so I'm stepping away from the basketball program at Fresno State for a few weeks. I hope to rejoin them soon. I want to thank the Bulldog fans, and I promise to come back and give them my best effort."

Shortly after I left the table in the front of the room, Tark spoke with tears in his eyes.

"We were going to send out a press release," he said, "but he wanted to come down here and face the media. This is very hard on me. Outside of my son, Danny, I might be closer to Chris than anyone I've ever coached."

I was on my way to a rehabilitation hospital in Salt Lake City. I felt so lost. I had run from Boston to get away from this, and now here I was in California with the same label. And this time it was all over ESPN.

I was in Utah for twenty-three days. I was one of the youngest people in rehab, if not the youngest, and I'd be in group-therapy sessions with guys with needle tracks on their arms, guys that had blown it all—jobs, families, everything—and they would look at me and shake their heads, as if to say, "What's wrong with you?" They couldn't understand why I would jeopardize everything I had, a potential NBA career and all the money that came with that. It was like they wanted to grab me and shake some sense into me.

A couple of times someone from the facility took me to a nearby gym and I'd shoot around for a while, but the season was going on without me.

By some strange quirk of fate, Peter Suneson's uncle, Mike Duscoe, was the director of the rehab facility. So in a sense I was protected. On my first day his wife gave me her ten-year sobriety medallion and told me that when I was sober for a year I could give it back to her. There was a lot of therapy, trying to get to the root of my problem. There was a lot of family stuff— my dad's drinking, the tension in the house. At one point both my parents came out, and we dealt with the drinking, the divorce, all of it.

I remember my father saying, "It's a devastating blow to watch your son in so much pain from three thousand miles away and not be able to help."

In many ways my stay in Utah was typical shit. Go to any rehab, and it's the same script. If you're young, you'll blame your parents.

I was no exception.

I was sitting in the room with the counselor and my parents.

"Dad, you drink too much."

"Mom, you work too much."

"You both fight too much."

I lashed out at them and took no responsibility for my own behavior.

When I retuned to Fresno three weeks later, Tark met me at the airport. We hugged.

"Chris called me every night," Tark told the media. "Sometimes we only talked for ten seconds, but he always called."

"It was a scary moment in my life," I told the media.

I also told them that I read the Bible every night, and when I woke up in the morning I felt better.

After Utah I was all right for a while. Maybe a few weeks. I told myself that the past was behind me, that I was on the road to recovery. I probably even believed it.

Then I went out again.

That's all it took.

Once I went out, I couldn't stop. Once I drank, there was a 90 percent chance I'd do cocaine. And once I started on coke, it was going to get ugly.

A couple of months later a writer from *Sports Illustrated* came out to do a story on me. His name was Gerry Callahan and now he's one of the cohosts on a very popular morning talk show in Boston. He was from Boston, he was a cool guy, and we hung out for a while.

"Herrren has been blessed with all the tools to play basketball at the highest level: the skills, the instincts, and a flair for the game," he wrote. "Coaches love him. Pro scouts rave about him. Fans adore him. The TV cameras can't get enough of him. He's a 6'3" guard who can shoot from NBA three-point range and slash to the hoop with rare quickness and power. He has a showman's love for the stage and a knack for coming through in the clutch. . . .

"His brown hair is streaked blond and his arms are covered with tattoos. He walks with a hip-hop swagger, talks in a too-cool cadence, and carries himself with the confidence of a rock star."

But I felt with Callahan that he knew it was all a con. I said all the right things, but it was like he knew me; he seemed to sense that I was a sinking ship.

That year a camera crew from Fox was following us around, filming a show that aired every Thursday night. It was called *Between the Madness,* and every time you turned around there was another camera in your face. One time they interviewed me about the future and all the other stuff I had absolutely no clue about.

"I think I might want to be an actor," I said.

Where did that come from?

Who knows.

But I was becoming an actor all right.

A bad one.

The Fox show was a look inside the circus tent, and we didn't disappoint.

Rafer Alston was a playground legend from New York City, where he was called "Skip to My Lou" for a signature dance-step maneuver he used to do with the ball in playground games. He had been to Fresno City junior college, and was on probation for assaulting an ex-girlfriend. Avondre Jones, a six-eleven center who was a rapper, lived in a cave of an apartment that was always dark and filled with what looked like skulls with candles coming out of them. Winfred Walton was six-nine and had started at Syracuse; his college board scores were challenged coming out of high school, and if you gave him the ball he was going to shoot it, no matter what was going on in the game or what the score was.

All of us were bizarre.

That's why we were there.

And it was always something. It was my rehab. It was Rafer getting suspended after being arrested for hitting his girlfriend. It was the constant failing of drug tests. It was Avondre and Kenny Brunner supposedly going after some guy with a samurai sword, another story that went out across the national wires like a shot in the dark.

And where was Tark in all this?

Tark was up in his office in his red Adidas sweat suit.

I felt sorry for him.

He was too old, and we were too crazy. It's hard enough running a Division I program, never mind trying to run a circus. He hadn't expected this—not to this extent, anyway. The more things happened, the more it began wearing on him. He'd put his hands on his head, his body language screaming out, "Not another one." It was *One Flew Over the Cuckoo's Nest* in baggy shorts and expensive sneakers, and every incident seemed to take more of the wind out of him.

"Chris," he would say to me. "Why are you doing that stuff? Is it really necessary?"

He didn't understand drugs, didn't understand that once you were addicted to them it was going to take more than willpower to stop. Tark wanted to defuse things. He couldn't understand the depths of our dysfunction, as if even after all the knuckle-heads he'd dealt with in the past he still wasn't ready for us.

One time, two players came into his office saying how another teammate had held a gun on them for a couple of hours. It seemed one of them had hooked up with the girlfriend of the guy with the gun, and he was threatening to kill them both. After a couple of hours he changed his mind and ran out of the apartment. The two players had been so terrified that they immediately ran to Tark.

"Coach," they said, "——— just held us hostage for a couple of hours."

Tark just looked at them.

"Let's see," he finally said. "You two guys are six foot seven, and ——— is six foot two, so if I were him, I'd have a gun, too. Get out of here and I'll see you at practice."

That was Coach Tark.

He was always trying to calm things down, get us back to what we were here for. It had all gotten so crazy that people were starting to have sympathy for him, even the people who didn't like him.

Someone was always getting in trouble, another guy with baggage coming to the team. My junior year we had Courtney Alexander sitting out, a transfer from Virginia, another big-time talent. He drove around the campus in his Lexus wearing gold chains and Rolexes, and I didn't like anything about him. But if you spin it, here was a guy who had a little daughter, who had already failed at Virginia, and he was trying to make it, too.

There were two sides to all of us: the one that was completely whacked, and the one that was trying to make a comeback, grab the brass ring as it went round and round.

And the flip side?

We went twenty-two and nine my first year, won the WAC title, and beat UMass when they were the number-nine team in the country, and Utah, with Keith Van Horn. We had nine guys in my time at Fresno who went on to play in NBA games.

But we didn't need a coach, we needed a psychiatrist.

Dominick Young and I went at each other a lot in practice that first year. He was crazy, volatile, very competitive, and every once in a while I'd get tired of his shit. But I respected his toughness, and basically we were all right together. I loved Terrance Roberson, but I never got along with Rafer. Yet I respected Rafer's work ethic, the way he worked at his game, something I wish I had done. Rafer was one of the great street players who could put all that away when he played for real. But we were in the semifinals of the NIT in Madison Square Garden that year and Rafer would never pass me the ball because he was back home and wanted to put on a show. I wasn't surprised.

Before that game in the Garden, while we were doing a shootaround, the only people in the building, in walks Mike Wallace.

Yeah, *that* Mike Wallace.

Two weeks earlier, a story had run on *60 Minutes* that had made us out to be what we were: the bad boys of Fresno State. Wallace had been out to Fresno, and it was sheer panic when he was there, because it was *60 Minutes* and Mike Wallace, and here they were in Fresno with reporters and producers who had been there for a couple of weeks and a camera crew. Then it runs and it's all there: my substance abuse, the samurai sword, the domestic abuse, the failed drug tests, the point-shaving allegations, all of it. I don't know what everyone expected. What did the school think they were going to get, a tribute to student athletes?

Wallace and I had spoken for nearly an hour, maybe twenty minutes on camera, forty minutes off. He was great with me. He talked about the Shah of Iran, John Kennedy, the Ayatollah, Massachusetts, all kinds of stuff. Kevin Mikolazyk and I hanging over the rail in the little campus gym talking to Mike Wallace; who would have ever believed that? It was a long way from talking to the guys on WSAR in Fall River after a Durfee game.

That I was on *60 Minutes* really meant nothing to me. But I was in awe of being in the company of Mike Wallace. He and *60 Minutes* were TV history, and I appreciated that.

And I couldn't understand why everyone in Fresno was so upset. He reported what his people gave him. I knew what it was, so I had expected the worst.

So here he comes into the Garden and he walks over to Tark, who was sitting on the bench.

"You fucked me," Tark said as Wallace sat down next to him.

Tark said it in his soft voice, showing no emotion.

"Jerry," Wallace said, immediately on the defensive.

"You fucked me," Tark said again, again showing no emotion, simply stating fact.

"Jerry," Wallace countered, obviously frustrated. "What did you expect? What did you expect me to do? What . . . ?"

"You fucked me," Tark said, staring straight ahead.

Wallace walked away, toward me.

I waved him off.

"Aw, Chris," he said.

But I walked away.

After the game he came into the locker room. He asked me if I wanted to go for dinner. I was so twisted and out of it I said no. Think about that for a second. Saying no to Mike Wallace.

But you know what?

If Mike Wallace had come out with me in New York back then, that clock on *60 Minutes* would never have stopped ticking.

That same spring, when we were in New York for the NIT, *Rolling Stone* magazine did a story called "Hoops and Misdemeanors." It was by a New York writer named Greg Donaldson, and he spent a few days in Fresno, including time at my apartment. Donaldson wrote:

"Fresno State is college basketball's heart of darkness—a volatile embodiment of both the best and the worst that high-powered sports programs have to offer. Rich in talent, with Chris Herren and six more high-school All-Americans, the Fresno State Bulldogs were ranked eighth in the country in a preseason survey by *Sports Illustrated* last November. But then the season broke out like a slow-motion riot: Herren was forced briefly into rehab, and the rest of the team racked up nine suspensions for everything from drug use to assault. The Bulldogs' reputation got so bad that at one point the *San Francisco Chronicle* suggested that the only place left for Latrell Sprewell to play was Fresno State."

Later the article said, "Part Montgomery Clift, part Jerry West, no individual player has ever seized the imagination of the city of Fresno like Chris Herren. He's got NBA talent, Hollywood glitter, and a blue-collar game that local fans fully understand.

"Making his way to class now, Herren hip-hops down the row of towering oaks and pine trees: He's wearing ankle-high motorcycle boots and an oversize blue sweater, and is perhaps the only white guy in America who doesn't look like an idiot in baggy jeans and a backward baseball cap. As he moves among the other students, no one is too insignificant for his personal attention. He nods to everyone and winks at, hugs or kisses the pretty coeds who drift toward him out of the fog. 'Did you do it yourself?' one of them asks, fingering his frosted hair."

My notoriety was growing, courtesy of some big games on national TV. Often the broadcast team was Len Elmore and Jimmy Dykes, and in the beginning of the season I had gone over and introduced myself. In a sense I played to the camera. Hit a big shot and nod your head. Not that I needed to. When I came back from rehab, every arena we went into people were all over me. The student section at SMU was chanting "Heroin" at me before I had ever done it.

Chris Heroin.

Over and over.

But you know what?

I fed off it.

I had always been a streaky player, an adrenaline player, and if I hit my first couple of jumpers, there was no stopping me. It was showtime.

That's what happened when we played at SMU. I'm going off, people are yelling everything they can think of, and I'm feeding off all of it, riding it. I am in the zone again, everything magnified, feeling that it's my game and I can do anything I want. At one point I hit a deep three right from the horse's mouth that was painted on the court, and Jimmy Dykes takes off his headset, stands, and bows in appreciation.

That only added to it.

By this time, I used all the yelling and screaming, all the verbal abuse, as fuel. It got so I played better on the road.

SMU was nothing compared to what happened every time we went to Hawaii, where I was the public enemy. I'd come through the tunnel and the whole arena would go nuts. People yelled, threw things, yelled some more. About point shaving. About rehab. "Fall River Nightmare." You name it, they yelled it. They hated me. And I'd blow kisses to them, which only made them crazier. As a sophomore I had kicked in thirty-five against them, in a game that all but ruined their season. After we beat them by two in an NIT quarterfinal game one year, some guy dumped a beer on my head.

When I went there my last time as a senior, there was a big story in the *Honolulu Star-Bulletin,* as if I were a folk hero.

"Tell them to show up," I was quoted about the fans. "I want to see ten thousand like I'm used to. I want to see the people who have been screaming at me the past two years."

"He plays with the crowd," Hawaii coach Riley Wallace said. "Most kids don't do that, but he acknowledges them and they feed off that. And he feeds off them. Might be better to give him the silent treatment."

They didn't.

But they threw leis on the court in appreciation, so in the end my teammates and I went on the plane wearing leis.

I loved Hawaii.

A couple of weeks later we hit New York City for the NIT like we were a rock group on tour. A story in the New York *Daily News* was called "Behind the Scenes with Tark's Circus Troupe." It said that we were either (a) the most corrupt crew of villains this side of a Dick Tracy comic strip, (b) the most misunderstood, media-maligned, unfairly treated group of fine young men you'd ever have the pleasure of meeting (see Fresno boosters, Jerry Tarkanian), or (c) the dopiest—oops, make that the hippest—collection of counterculture ballplayers anywhere.

Rafer was quoted as saying that we stank, that no one knew his role, and that our work ethic as a team was terrible.

"I keep hearing about how all these guys are considering leaving to go to the pros," Tark said. "Where are they going? Argentina? The CBA?"

We showed up with both Avondre Jones and Daymond Forney having been thrown off the team for failing drug tests, and so few guys available to play that we were practicing against opposing coaches and student managers.

We weren't a team anymore; we were a freak show.

I was quoted in the story, too.

"I shot the ball like two times all last summer. I was too busy partying. . . . Who am I to tell someone to stop smokin' weed. None of that affects me. I've got other things to worry about, like my sobriety."

Did I ever.

Kevin Mikolazyk, Gerry Landy, and Johnny Botelho, three friends from Fall River, had come out to stay with me at the end of my sophomore year. So much for getting out of Fall River. Fall River had come to me. It was Fall River West. It was also the biggest collection of knuckleheads you could put in any one apartment at any one time.

How fucked up was it?

I was the one with the most structure in his life. Think about that. At least I had practice to go to every day, and school once in a while. They didn't have anything to do except watch TV and sit around the pool every afternoon working on their tans, then wait for the night. We lived on my scholarship check, and money for housing because there were no dorms.

And when the season was over, Kevin and I started going to LA on weekends.

I had finished so strong that year, there was a school of

thought that I should enter the NBA draft, strike while the iron was hot, so to speak. It was appealing for a couple of reasons, one being that I knew I was doing major damage to my body, and maybe I could grab some money before it all blew up. I had agents and wannabe agents telling me they could get me money. But I was afraid of it, too, because I knew I wasn't ready, knew I was a fraud, that it was just a matter of time before I was discovered. But there were agents who said they could get me money, and that was seductive.

It was also the summer we discovered pain pills. Vicodin. Percocet. We were always going to hospital emergency rooms on the ride to LA trying to get some pills. We told them anything. Toothache. Any kind of ache. Sometimes we'd hit three or four on the ride, anything to get fucked up, out of our heads. Kevin was a master at getting drugs this way. He looked about sixteen, with a sweet, choirboy face, and people couldn't say no to him.

We stayed with a guy in Santa Monica who was trying to be an agent, and sometimes there'd be a couple of grand in the nightstand when we got there. We'd go out to the hot clubs, places where all the starlets and wannabe starlets were hanging out. We were living like we had money when we didn't. It was a long way from hanging out in the McDonald's parking lot in Fall River. But we could party with anyone. We'd end up at parties in the Hollywood hills, end up everywhere. Once, we were at the restaurant where the movie *Get Shorty* had been filmed.

And there were nights we'd be at a swanky rooftop restaurant ordering stuff off the menu that we had never heard of, ordering stuff with someone else's money, two little knuckleheads from Fall River who had no fuckin' clue what they were doing.

■CHAPTER EIGHT■

In June 1999 I was the thirty-third pick in the NBA draft.

Complete with a party to celebrate it.

It was in Fall River, in a club down by the waterfront, and to get to it there was a police escort for Heather and me from our apartment near Ruggles Park to the Coliseum, where five hundred people were waiting, including my parents, my brother, all my friends, Mr. Karam, and six television stations. Many of the people had been there for a couple of hours. In many ways it was a big city party. Basketball in Fall River had been so important for so long, since the late 1940s when Durfee had won the state championship in the old Boston Garden, and this was the first time anyone had ever been drafted by the NBA. But I was too young and too dumb to realize the symbolic nature of the whole thing because I was overwhelmed with anxiety.

That night was the culmination of many things, certainly, but it had really begun after the Fresno season died, in a first-round loss in the NIT in a game at the University of California in Berkeley. That had been it for me in Fresno. I was done. I was out of there, even though I lacked the credits to graduate.

Heather and I had been married the summer before, soon after Heather found out she was pregnant. The irony was that we had broken up earlier that summer, because that was our history together. We were always breaking up, then getting back together, over and over. It had been going on since we were twelve years old.

I had come back to Fall River after the NIT my junior year and we had reconnected. I still wasn't ready to be the guy she deserved, and we had another fight.

"I can't do this anymore, Chris," she said. "There's too much heartbreak."

She had graduated from Providence College and was working as a waitress in Newport, trying to decide what she was going to do with her life, and she said that all this back-and-forth with me had simply become too difficult for her, that I had turned her life upside down too many times.

I really thought she was done.

A week later I was flying back to Fresno with Kevin.

"I think I've fucked up the best thing that's ever happened to me," I said to him.

About six weeks later the phone rang one afternoon.

It was Heather.

I was thrilled. I thought I had lost her.

"How are you doing?" she asked.

"I'm doing okay."

We made small talk for a few minutes.

"You need to know I'm late," she said.

"No problem. Give me a call later," I said, thinking she was late for work.

"No," she said. "I'm late, late."

I took a deep breath.

"Are you sure?"

She laughed.

She said she'd go to the drugstore and take a test, then call me.

"I'm pregnant," she said when she called back.

She cried.

I cried.

There was not one piece of me that didn't want to marry her.

"It looks like I'm coming home," I said.

We got married in August at a church in Somerset, Massachusetts, the town across the river from Fall River, where Heather had grown up. The reception was at the Fall River Country Club. One hundred and fifty people were invited. Three hundred showed up. The bar eventually ran out of beer. Then we went to the Coliseum and they ran out of beer, too.

We were supposed to go to Cape Cod the next day for our honeymoon, to a ritzy resort called the Chatham Bars Inn. But not only didn't we know what the Chatham Bars Inn was, we didn't know the way to the Cape. We were two kids with no clue. I had to call my father and ask him how to get to the Cape, even though it was only an hour away.

Then we went back to Fresno for my senior year.

My life was 180 degrees different that year. Things had calmed down, major. I dabbled once in a while with painkillers—Vicodin and Percocet—but for the most part I was good. I was off cocaine, which had had a serious depressive effect on me. We lived in a condo, and by my standards it was very normal. We even adopted a dog, a black Lab named Miles. Heather knew that I went out once in a while and did some things I shouldn't be doing. She knew that after I drank I wanted to do cocaine. She knew that I got out of control sometimes. She had witnessed that. But she had no idea of the extent of my addiction. I never allowed her to see that back then, never wanted to live that life around her. So that year I was only an occasional user. I hadn't developed an everyday habit. I didn't have the money for it, and I rarely went out.

Again, we had a very talented team at Fresno State. Again, we had problems—not as severe and as well-publicized as the year before, but problems nonetheless. I was exclusively a point guard that year, the position that at only six foot two I would have to play in the NBA, but a severe ankle injury early in the year knocked me out of several games and bothered me much of the season. Once again we underachieved as a team, failing to get to the NCAA tournament, and once again I felt sorry for Tark. He had had such big dreams. Going back to Fresno. Repeating his success at UNLV in Fresno. One more great ride. And they were all being blown up by us, all of us with our big reputations and total dysfunction. All of us chasing the basketball dream that had more to do with one day making the NBA and making money than it did about winning games for Fresno, however sad that sounds now.

That year it had become all about the NBA, showcasing myself for it, trying to settle on an agent, trying to take basketball to another level. My mother and grandfather flew out for "Senior Day," and that was a very emotional time. The people in Fresno had been unbelievably kind to me. I don't think there was any better place I could have played than Fresno. The building was always electric, the same people in the same seats, game after game, and I got to know them. I never could have found a more supportive place. For all my troubles there, and all the controversies I was involved in, there was never a negative moment from those people. The people in Fresno stayed with me the whole way. Through everything that happened in the four years there, the point-shaving allegations, my stint in rehab, everything, they gave me the benefit of the doubt. They loved me and I loved them.

And now it was ending.

It had been four years at the other end of the country, four years that no one could have ever made up, including me.

I had come close to hiring Dan Fegan as my agent. He was young, on the rise, very aggressive, and we had struck up a great relationship. He also recognized my problems, and once said that if he was going to be my agent we were first and foremost going to address my issues, and that if I didn't deal with things off the court I wasn't going to be on the court very long. In the end, I think that steered me away from him, because I was afraid of that.

Instead, I signed with Frank Catapano, who was older, in his fifties, from Boston. He had been an agent for a long time, representing such Boston-area players as John Bagley and Dana Barros. He was very friendly with Leo Papile from BABC, and Mikey Martin, who had played with Michael at Durfee, was working for him. So it all felt comfortable.

Nothing else did.

Showcasing yourself for NBA teams is extremely nerve-wracking.

How relaxed do you think you'd be working out in front of Pat Riley, with all his NBA title rings and his star power?

And I had been in college for five years and didn't have a degree. I had a wife. I had a child. What else was a guy like me going to do? To say your ass is on the line working out for NBA teams is an understatement.

The drill was always the same when you worked out for teams, whether it was Miami, Indiana, Atlanta, or Denver, the four I worked out for, though I also interviewed with the Clippers. Before working out for the teams there was an invitational tournament in Phoenix where you went for the better part of a week and played before a whole shitload of scouts. Maybe forty to fifty players were there, all considered late-first-round to second-round guys. It was three days of workouts and games, and it was a big test for me. It was different from playing in Fresno.

Can I play with different guys?

Can I play the point against this kind of competition, since I had only played it one year in college?

These were the unanswered questions, both for me and for the scouts.

The workouts for individual teams were different. You'd fly into the city the night before, go out to dinner with the coaches, an unofficial interview. The next day you'd have the workouts. Dribble drills. Shooting from spots. Catch and shoot. Then shoot off one dribble, off two dribbles. Usually there were two or three other guys with you, so you're all competing with one another, yet you're all in the same boat, too, so there's a certain camaraderie. Several times I was with Vonteego Cummings of Pittsburgh and John Celestand of Villanova. We were all combo guards in college who were now trying to convince teams that we could be point guards in the NBA. Miami was the hardest workout; Riley had the reputation of killing guys once the doors opened and the lights came on. Denver was the most relaxed.

Before the workouts I had gone to Indianapolis to stay with basketball great Chris Mullin, who had taken an interest in me.

Mullin had been one of the most celebrated college players ever, being named Big East Player of the Year three times while playing for St. John's in the mid 1980s. He was one of the greatest players ever to come out of New York City, a megastar. He played in the NBA for sixteen years, at one point averaging at least twenty-five points a game for five straight years, and played on two Olympic teams, including the 1992 Dream Team. He was at the tail end of his career in the spring of 1999, then playing for the Indianapolis Pacers. Along the way he, too, had battled his own well-publicized alcohol addiction.

So what was our original connection, besides addiction issues?

Steve Nash, the great point guard for the Phoenix Suns.

Nash had played at Santa Clara in college, and Fresno had played Santa Clara the year I sat out, so we knew each other and had the "two white guys" thing going on. He was friendly with Mullin.

"Do me a favor," he said to Mullin. "Take him in for a while to get him ready for the predraft camps."

The Pacers also had an interest in me, some of it based on the fact that my agent, Frank Catapano, and the Pacers' general manager, Donnie Walsh, were very friendly.

So there I was one day in Mullin's kitchen. He was busy, with four kids, trying to get ready for another season. I felt like I was intruding. Plus I was in awe of him. I'd had his picture hanging on my bedroom wall when I was a kid. I remember cutting out a picture of him in a magazine and adding it to my collage of great players.

We touched on our addiction issues then, but we didn't dive in. He was too big a figure for me at the time. If anything, I was closer to his wife, Liz. She was very compassionate about everything, and seemed to understand me. Right from the beginning she was like my big sister. I was in Indianapolis for maybe a week and a half, living in a small condo and working out with Mullin maybe five times, when the call came that Heather was back in Fall River getting ready to give birth, three weeks early.

That afternoon I was holding Christopher in Charlton Memorial Hospital, staring at this newborn, at the wonder of him, at how unbelievable it was.

I couldn't wrap my head around having a child.

No big surprise.

I couldn't wrap my head around anything.

It was as if my life was on speed dial.

Married.

A new father.

Auditioning for NBA teams.

My future up in the air.

It was an incredibly anxious time, not just for me, but for everyone. My father was quoted saying that it had been a long, long ride, and that he could see the strain on me. My mother was quoted saying that she really didn't care about the NBA.

"I just hope and pray that Christopher finds some peace in his life," she said.

On the day of the draft, my brother was on his radio show on WSAR.

"Tonight is the night," he kept saying over and over, "and my brother is a nervous wreck."

I was asked if playing in the NBA had been my childhood dream.

"My dream was to play for Durfee," I said. "That was my dream."

But Michael had been right. I was a nervous wreck. I knew I was real close to the NBA. I felt that if I hadn't had my troubles

I would definitely have been a first-round pick, but I knew I was tainted.

"I am what I am," I told one reporter that afternoon. "It happened. It's in the past."

Tough talk, but inside I was all nerves.

But hearing my name announced on draft night in June 1999 was unbelievable. I thought I might go to Indiana at the twenty-fifth pick in the first round, but they took Vonteego Cummings instead. Then after the first round ended, Denver's coach, Dan Issel, called.

"Congratulations," he said. "We're happy to have you as a Nugget."

It was just Heather and me in the apartment when it happened, and all of a sudden you've been drafted by the NBA, and all you can think of is how utterly amazing that is, how just five years earlier you had been at Durfee and hanging out in Suneson's basement, and the biggest game in the world was against New Bedford, and now you were going to the NBA.

Complete with the party to prove it.

It was great, a big Fall River celebration, complete with a band. It had come with a certain suspense, the disappointment growing in the room as the end of the first round wound down and I hadn't been drafted yet. At least that's what the newspaper article said the next morning. Everyone was waiting to celebrate, like it was about to be midnight on New Year's Eve, and the clock had stopped at two minutes to twelve. Then the draft show went to a commercial, and when it came back it said that

Denver had selected Fresno State guard Chris Herren with the thirty-third pick.

The crowd exploded, and Michael, who was running the whole night, jumped up and down in ecstasy.

"Let's party!" he shouted to the crowd.

About a half hour later Heather and I came down Anawan Street in our light blue Jeep Cherokee, complete with police escort. There was a big poster on the wall that had my face against the backdrop of the Braga Bridge. It was like a scene out of some Hollywood movie: local boy makes good and the whole town is proud.

And the next morning Heather and I were on the plane to Denver, where James Posey, a swingman from Xavier who had been the Nuggets' first pick, and I were introduced as the newest members of the Nuggets.

Dan Issel, the Nuggets coach, had been a college star at Kentucky, and then a great pro with the Nuggets. He was huge, maybe six foot nine, and his nickname was "Horse." He had blond hair that was going gray, and traces of his Southern roots in his speech.

At the workout in Denver before the draft we had taken a ride, and he asked me some questions abut my drug use. I thought he understood my background and how I had grown up. He wanted to help me. He was wonderful with me, a great person. He was a straight shooter, a regular guy. There was never any pretense about him. Everyone liked Dan Issel. His door was always open. He had told me that they had an early pick in the second round and if I was still on the board they were going to take me, which had taken some of the pressure off. But you never know. I was a realist. I had been labeled. Everyone knew about my issues, and if I had been a general manager I probably wouldn't have taken me.

When I got to Denver in the fall, the message was very clear: there was to be no drinking for me. Denver was full of quality guys, veterans like George McCloud, Popeye Jones, Antonio McDyess, Roy Rogers. They watched out for me from the beginning. They couldn't have been better. Chauncey Billups took me to his house and gave me some of his suits. Popeye Jones took me shopping.

Why shopping?

They no doubt looked at my jeans and Chuck Taylors and my hat on backward and said there's no way this kid is ready for the NBA.

My wardrobe was a long way from Prada shoes and linen pants.

McDyess had a platinum bracelet filled with diamonds that he knew I liked, and the next year when I was in Boston he came into the locker room before the Nuggets were to play the Celtics.

"I have something for you," he said, giving me an envelope.

In it was the bracelet.

Which I would later hock, of course.

But that year in Denver they were all like big brothers to me. I had already spent some time that summer with the Nuggets in a summer league in Salt Lake City. NBA summer league is full of rookies, young NBA players, and guys hoping to get invited to veterans' camp in the fall. It's extremely cutthroat; everyone's trying to impress, to land one of the few coveted spots in the NBA. Everyone's under the gun.

One of the guys it was hard on was Cory Alexander, who had played for the Nuggets the year before. He had played at the University of Virginia, had been in the league for four years, and was the backup for Nick Van Exel. Now there was this second-round draft choice coming after that role. He could have been brutal with me. Instead, he was great, extremely helpful, even though we were competing for the same spot. That's the thing about the NBA, something that's usually overlooked. One guy's going up, and the other guy's going down. Everyone's riding the wave.

It's incredibly stressful, especially for the guys either trying to make the league or hang on in the league. It's not stressful for the guys with the huge guaranteed contracts. But it is for everyone else. The line between who makes it and who doesn't is a very thin one.

Denver was a clean year for me, a wonderful year. The NBA. Serious money, $320,000, complete with side money for signing basketball cards. I ran my own basketball camp at Durfee the summer before, which was packed. To people in Fall River I was a hero, the kid who had gone from the Durfee field house all the way to the NBA.

We lived in a condo about eight minutes away from the Pepsi Center, the new downtown arena where the Nuggets both played and practiced. I was driving a new $36,000 black Ford Explorer. But I didn't buy fancy suits. I didn't buy jewelry. That wasn't me, had never been me, and was never going to be me. But you're living better, no question about it. You eat in better restaurants. You eat better steak. You've got money in your pocket. On the road you're staying in five-star hotels.

Life was great.

The biggest adjustment?

Understanding your role in the NBA.

You're expected to act like an adult. You're expected to act like you're in corporate America. You're expected to be places on time, work hard when you're there, and do things the right way. That's why there's so much turnover in the NBA, because too many young players don't understand that; they think it's just about basketball. But it's about a whole lot more than that. The bench guys who hang around the league for a long time are the ones who get it.

Then you have to adjust to the NBA game. In college I could get to the rim maybe 80 percent of the time. In the NBA it was probably 20 percent of the time. Instead of maybe one six-foot-eleven guy waiting for you when you get to the rim, there might be three, six hands up there to try to block your shot instead of two. Your game gets pushed further out. You have to adjust, and you have to do it quickly. And you've got to realize that you're not the man. You're like the walk-on on a college team, the kid without the scholarship. You might get four minutes in a half to get it done, and that's if you're fortunate. I was a backup point guard, so my job was to come in for Nick Van Exel and keep pushing the tempo. Push the ball and don't turn it over. You also have to learn to not let it psychologically crush you when you miss your first shot. You have to learn to deal with coming in and turning the ball over right away. You can't let these things start playing with your head, make you tentative, or else you're done right from the start. It's more a mind game than anything else, figuring out what you can do and what you can't, figuring out how you're going to fit. You're on a short leash.

There was no one defining moment when I knew I could play in the NBA. I had played well in the rookie league in Utah. There had been a couple of preseason games I played well in. I simply began to feel more comfortable with the speed of the NBA game, the size of it.

Van Exel was a big help.

He had been in the league for six years, a six-foot-one slithery point guard who could score. I remember sitting on my couch as a kid watching him play for Cincinnati in college and loving his game. In the beginning he was very standoffish and aloof with me, though. He was tough. He had seen a lot of guys come through training camp in his time. But once he knew I was going to be around, he was great. And he had big balls. It was in his blood to make big shots. Outside of Kobe Bryant, he might have made as many big shots as anyone back then. You'd be surprised how many guys, even great ones, run from taking big shots. Nick never did.

On one of the first plane trips, I was playing a card game

called Boo Ray. I was young and dumb, and I saw big dollars right in front of me. Before I knew it, I was down eight grand, and then when the game ended I was down $16,000. The drill is, you write a check, give it to the guy who won, done deal.

But I didn't have a checkbook, and I probably had $400 in my pocket.

Plus, I was sick to my stomach.

Later that night, Van Exel called me to his room.

"Don't worry," he said, giving me a wink. "I got it covered."

One of the assistant coaches was John Lucas, who had been a great college player at the University of Maryland in the 1970s, and a star guard in the NBA before his own well-publicized troubles with cocaine addiction. I knew his story, and I liked him a lot. He was trying to help me, wanted to go for coffee. On the road he would sometimes wake me up early to go to a meeting. But I didn't recognize my addiction yet. I still wanted to believe that beer was my friend, that I could go out and be social, blow a few lines every once in a while, even though I did very little of that when I was in Denver. But that was still my mind-set, like I had a problem that had gone away for a while. It still had never really been dealt with. It was like a sleeping giant.

In one of my first games we were playing the Houston Rockets and Vernon Maxwell was guarding me when I checked into the game, my nerves almost jumping through my skin. We had the ball out of bounds and the play was for me to come off a screen.

"Listen to me," Maxwell said. "There's two seconds on the

shot clock. I'm not going to chase you, so go off that screen and knock that jumper down."

So I come off the screen, catch the ball, and hurriedly throw up a shot.

Air ball.

And there's Maxwell laughing at me and pointing at the clock, which said there were twenty-three seconds left.

People think that the NBA is diamonds, platinum, videos, limousines, and bottles of champagne. That's really very little of it. Mostly it's living out of a suitcase. Life on the road is taking the bus to the plane, then to the hotel, then to the shootaround, then to the game, then back to the plane.

The only bad night was in Miami. One night before a game with the Heat we went to a strip club called Rolex. It was in the ghetto, one of those places featured in rap videos. Van Exel was there. James Posey. George McCloud. A few other players. I was the only white guy in the club, but it was cool. People were throwing money around; it got lively. I felt totally comfortable until another white guy walked in, and it started to get real uncomfortable for me. He was acting goofy, drawing attention to himself. The vibe was changing. Eventually, I went to another club with a few other guys, and I got crazy, and it got crazy, and when I got back to the hotel at five thirty in the morning there was a message to call George McCloud.

"What are you doing?" he said on the phone.

I felt awful, like I was letting him down.

And the other message?

This is a business.

That was the lesson the older guys taught me—McCloud, McDyess, Rogers, Van Exel—that beneath all the cheers and the five-star hotels, beneath all the charter flights and the checks that came twice a month and had big numbers on them, basketball was a cold-hearted business.

"There's the front office and there's the locker room," Van Exel would say, "and the two have nothing in common. It's not one big happy family here. You're on one side, and they're on the other. They can pull your card anytime they want. So I don't want to be the guy cashing the checks. I want to be the guy signing them."

You soon learned that the NBA is a carousel; guys jump off, guys jump on. Some guys figure out the politics of it. Some guys don't. That's life. I was smart enough to understand it, but too dumb to apply that understanding.

You also soon learned that there were rules for the stars, and different rules for you. I could drive to the basket against the Lakers and Shaq would all but take my head off. No foul. Van Exel could skip down the lane, not even get touched, throw up a shot that missed, and it was a foul. That was just the way it was. Everyone knew it. That, and the way the stars could talk to the referees, saying virtually anything to them with no retribution.

A ref would make a call against Van Exel.

"What the fuck was that?" he'd say to the ref. "What's wrong with you? Make the call, motherfucker."

The NBA was often a game within a game.

Like the time I came into a game and was matched up against Allen Iverson.

"Get loose," he said to me. "I'll give you two minutes before I come at you."

The worst thing you could do was get the stars mad, make it so they wanted to take it to you. So much of the NBA then was isolation, you against someone else one-on-one, and for me, the two guys I least wanted to see with the ball were Iverson and Stephon Marbury on the wing and me guarding them with no help. Iverson was Houdini-quick, and Marbury was both quick and strong. Even if you were still with him after his first step, he'd lower his shoulder and bump you off him. So you didn't want to get those guys riled up, make it personal. I'd see what Van Exel would do when guys tried to make it personal with him. His eyes would light up. He'd bring them inside and torch them. I'd see McDyess, who is the quietest, sweetest guy in the world. Then some guy would make it personal with him, and you could see the beast in him wake up.

Issel was great with me.

He had started the season with me on injured reserve. I think that was his way of getting me adjusted to the league, to let me sit there and watch for a while, get acclimated. When I made my first shot in a real game, he had a big smile on his face, and when I came to the bench, he gave me a big hug.

"Keep your head up," he would constantly tell me.

That was his message.

If I played well he'd high-five me.

If I didn't?

"Keep pushing," he'd say. "It's a long season. You're going to be fine."

Everyone got along. Everyone liked Issel. There was the sense that Denver was a team on the upswing. I had my moments. In one game against the Wizards, one of my sneakers came off and the game kept going, so there was I with one shoe on and one off, and the ball came to me on the right side and I made a three, and it was CNN's "Play of the Day," repeated endlessly for about twenty-four hours. I had eighteen against Dallas in a game where Van Exel had been hurt and didn't play and I had gotten a lot of minutes. I had games when I played well, and I had games when I didn't, but when you're a backup point guard coming off the bench it's not about you. You are in the game to make your teammates better, to get them the ball in the right places at the right time.

At the end of the season I knew I could play in the league.

I could get the ball by people. I was more comfortable running the pick-and-roll, more familiar with the defensive schemes. Most important, my confidence was up.

And when it ended, Heather and I went back to Fall River.

That's the other thing about the NBA: it can be very hard on families. I was gone half the year playing on the road and Heather would be stuck in Denver with a one-year-old. She didn't have a lot of friends. She missed her family. It was the second year she had been on the other side of the country from her parents and it was a big adjustment for her. So when the season ended, we couldn't wait to get back home.

In retrospect, it was a big mistake. I should have seen Denver as our new home. I was under contract for another year, on a team that seemed to like me, and the mature thing would have been to stay there that summer, work out every day at the Nuggets' practice facility, treat the NBA like the year-round job it should be. If I had figured that out, worked hard, watched a lot of film, gotten in great shape, done all those things, I might have had a ten-year career. Instead, I felt like a kid who couldn't wait for summer vacation.

So we came back to Fall River.

I was in the NBA, I was about to make nearly half a million dollars in my second year, I was married to the love of my life, and if you looked at me that summer, with my own basketball camp, driving around in my black Ford Explorer, money in my pocket, you would have thought I had the perfect life.

You would have thought wrong.

■CHAPTER NINE■

In October 2000 I was introduced at a press conference as the newest member of the Boston Celtics, one of a handful of New England guys who had ever played for the Celtics.

The Celtics were everything when I was a kid. I idolized them. When I was out in the driveway with the spotlight on the basket, playing imaginary games in my head, the shot clock ticking off while I made the big shot to win the game, I was Danny Ainge, Larry Bird. Every ball I bounced, every shot I took, it was always about the Celtics. My father had taken me and my brother to a big rally in Government Center in Boston in 1986 when they won the title. I was eleven years old. I even had an autographed picture of Larry Bird, which said, "To Chris, keep playing," signed on a place mat from a Boston bar that my father and his cronies used to frequent.

But that day at the press conference none of that mattered. That day should have been one of the highlights of my life.

Instead, it's all a blur, half-remembered, if remembered at all. My life was much too painful by then. Everything was about just trying to get through the day and keep the lie going, because the reality was that by the time I got to the Celtics, I was hooked on OxyContin.

I started getting into opiates that summer, when Heather and I left Denver for what was supposed to be a happy summer with our baby, Chris, in Fall River. Actually, I had started in my junior year at Fresno after I came back from rehab, and was getting off cocaine. I'd always hated cocaine, even when I was using it, hated coming down from it, the depression, the empty feeling. Cocaine brought me to a point where I couldn't look at myself. Vicodin was different. Vicodin was mellow. It slowed things down. And for some reason, I could play basketball on it. The first few times it made me sleepy and tired me out, but after a while it was like a pep pill. Kevin Mikolazyk and I were chasing it everywhere, "med-seeking" from emergency room to emergency room. Eventually, we had to pull back the reins, because it was becoming constant chaos, complete with NyQuil to go to sleep.

But in the summer of 2000 I discovered OxyContin.

It was the first time OxyContin had been in Fall River, and I began using it.

Why did I take it?

That's the million-dollar question.

Was it just my insecurities, fears, anxieties?

Was it my addictive personality that had never been dealt with, even if I had lived a fairly clean year in Denver?

Was it the fact I never had felt comfortable in my own skin and still didn't, even if on the surface it seemed like I was living some dream life?

Was it all of the above?

Whatever it was, if drugs were around, odds were I was going to take them.

If it was cocaine, I was going to snort it. If it was acid, I was going to drop it. If it was painkillers, I was going to chew them. If it was mushrooms, I was going to eat them. I wasn't saying no very often. It was like getting all fucked up the night before the CBS game against UMass in Fresno my junior year. Couldn't I have just taken that night off and stayed home? It was like playing for the WAC championship one year in Hawaii when I spent the night before the game in a strip club. Couldn't I have stayed in the hotel that one night?

That was the insanity of it.

And if I started putting substances in my body, I couldn't stop. That had always been the case, and it wasn't any different now.

OxyContin began as a pain medicine for cancer patients, a very powerful narcotic. Now it had become a street drug, as kids were getting it from people who were dying of HIV, dying of horrible things like pancreatic cancer. You weren't taking Vicodin, something that people with toothaches were taking. Or Percocet, what people with bad backs were taking. You were taking painkillers that people with terminal illnesses were taking.

You were crossing a line.

I knew they were the most powerful things I had ever put in my body. I knew I shouldn't be taking them.

I took them anyway.

They came in a pack of four little pills in different colors, all increasing in strength. The 20 milligrams were pink. The 40 milligrams were yellow. The 80 milligrams were green. And the 160 milligrams were blue. From the beginning, OxyContin made me feel comfortable in my own skin, and I went strong at it. Alcohol made me angry and aggressive. Cocaine made me severely depressed. OxyContin made me mellow. It took the edge off, took away the anxiety. I was able to trick myself into thinking I was better off taking it, that it was helping me.

My friend and I called them "Scooby snacks," like they were some little kid's thing.

"Got any Scooby snacks?"

Like they were no big deal.

But very soon my whole world depended on them. They were $50 a pill, and I started off at two pills a day, but that soon became a $500-a-day habit, then more.

That's when the nightmare began.

I soon knew I was in trouble. I couldn't be without it. Some mornings I would wake up in the fetal position, sweating when it was cold, shivering when it was hot. And when that happened, the only thing that would fix it was more pills.

The chase was on.

I continued to work out that summer, only not as hard as the summer before, doing it to keep people off my back. I ran another summer camp at Durfee that was very successful. I signed basketball cards for money. I had a deal with Reebok, a Massachusetts sneaker company. It was all part of another smoke and mirrors act, only this time the act was coming home and in the middle of the biggest spotlight I ever could have envisioned.

I've seen pictures of that press conference when I first came to Boston, but I don't remember what I said. I do remember that it was a big story in both the *Globe* and the *Herald* and on TV, the fact that I had been a two-time Massachusetts high school player of the year, and now I was coming home to play for the Celtics, part of a deal that sent Bryant Stith and me to the Celtics for Robert Pack and Calbert Cheaney in a low-level NBA trade. What a great story it was.

I also remember Rick Pitino invited Heather and me to his town house on Commonwealth Avenue in Boston, not far from Boston Common, for lunch.

He talked about the guys he had coached before, guys I could pattern myself after. He talked a lot about motivation, and that if I bought into what he was saying it could do great things for me, that all I had to do was buy into it. He was very positive, talked about the great opportunity there was for me in Boston. But I felt awkward, too, intimidated by the lifestyle he had. The catered lunch. The fact he had both a wine cellar and a movie theater in his house. Rick Pitino would have been overpowering if he'd been sitting in a living room in Fall River, never mind in a Boston town house.

And my head was already in a bad place.

I like Pitino. He was always good to me. But he was in his fourth year in Boston then, and it wasn't living up to the promise. He had arrived with so much attention, so many expectations, with a national championship at Kentucky on his résumé. He was going to make the Celtics the Celtics again, bring back the glory days of Bird and Kevin McHale and Robert Parish in the 1980s when the old Garden rang with cheers, and the Celtics and the Lakers were NBA royalty, Bird and the Lakers' Magic Johnson taking the league to new heights of popularity. There had been a huge press conference on the floor of the Fleet Center when he'd been formally announced, complete with all the banners in the rafters brought down to floor level, all the great Celtics history behind him. It hadn't been just a press conference. It had been like a coronation. He was the hottest college coach in the country, he had NBA experience, both as an assistant coach and as a head coach with the Knicks, he had played at UMass and coached at Boston University, and at the time he seemed like the perfect guy to be the new Celtics coach.

But here they were, just another young team going nowhere, in a league full of them. He was under tremendous pressure. He was Rick Pitino, one of the biggest names in basketball, and he was supposed to win.

But by the time I got traded, I was happy for all the wrong reasons. I wasn't happy because I was back home and had grown up idolizing the Celtics.

I was happy because I was back home and I knew where to get drugs. I also had the money to buy them.

It was a deadly combination.

Even then, it was beginning to feel like a minute-to-minute life, but I could fool the shit out of people. I was afraid of help. But I could function, too. Even fake it through a press conference. Everything revolved around keeping the lie going.

Before I could officially join the Celtics, they had me go down to the University of Florida on the sly to work out with Billy Donovan. He was the coach of Florida, but he had played for Rick Pitino at Providence College, the star of a team that had somehow gotten to the Final Four in 1987, and he had also been an assistant with Pitino at Kentucky, the one who had been involved in recruiting me. So he and I had a relationship. And Donovan was doing Pitino a favor.

And now Pitino was telling me through my agent to go work out with Donovan.

The only problem was that my habit was getting worse.

I had been taking OxyContin every day, and now I didn't have it.

Try getting through a Billy Donovan workout when you feel great, never mind when you're sick as a dog and aren't sure you're going to be able to get out of bed in the morning, let alone play basketball.

Work out in the gym.

Then on the treadmill, where you had to go hard.

Back to the gym.

Back on the treadmill.

Back to the gym.

Back on the treadmill.

This was the day.

Pitino's entire basketball philosophy was based on being the better conditioned team, the team that was going to outwork the opponent, be more aggressive, get more deflections, create the pace of the game. It's the style he'd made his reputation on, first at Providence College in 1987 when he was the national coach of the year, in his two years with the Knicks right after that, and then during his time at Kentucky, when he won a national championship in 1996.

His approach with players was simple: lose weight.

He was obsessed with a player's weight, wanted everyone to be as thin as they could be.

The two stars the Celtics were banking on were Antoine Walker, who had played for Pitino at Kentucky for two years, and Paul Pierce, then in his third year in the league. They were both young players, but they were different, too. Pierce was very hardworking. You could see he wanted to be great. He came to practice early and stayed late. Some days I'd be coming to practice, arriving often at the last possible minute, and he'd already be drenched in sweat. Paul was a regular guy, likeable. Antoine thought of himself as the leader, thought of the Celtics as his team. He was showy, liked to be the man, from his famous wiggle on the court after he made a big play, to coming into some club on the road and throwing a couple of grand on the table where a few of us would be sitting and letting us see him spend it.

Then again, he once said that he "wiped his ass with hundred-dollar bills."

I sometimes thought that he was jealous of all the attention I got, all the hometown stuff, but maybe that was just my own sensitivity. Whatever, we never really clicked. But one time when I needed money he gave me $5,000, so it was complicated. He was a young player in the league who was being asked to be a leader, and he wasn't really ready for the role. That wasn't his fault. Unlike Denver, which had a lot of veteran leaders, we had none. Our highest-paid guys were young guys, and that's not good.

Kenny Anderson used an alias on the road. It was the name of the guy who had taken care of him at Georgia Tech. He had drinking issues, liked the social scene. And he had money issues, astronomical child support payments.

Vitaly Potapenko was a regular guy, the Ukraine Train. He was six foot nine with a shaved head, and looked like he could be an enforcer in the Russian mob. A tough, blue-collar type, he wasn't afraid of the black guys, and no one fucked with him.

In one of his first practices with the Celtics he had gotten into a beef with Mark Blount.

"You mess with me," he said, "and I will skull fuck you."

No one messed with him after that, although he and Blount didn't like each other and were constantly going at each other in practice. Then again, they were playing the same position, competing with each other for playing time.

Vitaly liked his Amstel Lights. We'd be on the plane coming

in somewhere and he'd be calling the hotel and telling them to have two filet mignons and two six-packs of Amstel Lights in his room when he got there. It was one of the reasons we got along: we both liked to drink on the road, hang out.

In many ways it was a miserable year, and not just for me. The players weren't happy. There was no real leadership. It was like a spending contest. Who pulled into the parking lot with the best car. Who went to the best clubs. In Denver, guys wanted other guys to succeed. With the Celtics it was who could get the most out of it. Pitino tried, but it was very difficult. It's one thing when you're winning. Guys will buy into what you're selling when you're winning. But when you're losing you lose power, and Pitino was losing. When you're losing players start questioning the coach more. His technique. How long he practices. Everything. Very soon it was like Pitino was walking around with the weight of the world on his shoulders. I didn't just walk into the coach's office like I could in Denver. He was always busy.

But I didn't hang out with guys in Boston like I did in Denver. Because the only way I could keep my lie going was to isolate myself from people, not let anyone get too close.

"Chris Herren finds his dream—and renewed strength—in return to his roots," read the subhead in a huge centerpiece story in the *Boston Herald* under a big headline in bold type that said, "Home Court Advantage."

That story came out around Thanksgiving. It was written by Mark Cofman and included pictures of me at Durfee, a picture of me guarding Antoine Walker in the McDonald's game, and a game picture of me in a Celtics uniform with the ball in my left hand and holding up two fingers in my right hand. It said how I'd become an unlikely starter after Kenny Anderson had broken his jaw and was out for a while.

"What Chris has done is not easy," Pitino was quoted as saying. "He missed half of training camp before the trade and spent the first five games of the season inactive. He was losing a lot of weight at the time because we had asked that of him, and then he's thrown right into the fire when he returns. He's done a remarkable job of handling everything.

"I love his energy, his work ethic, and his commitment. This young man has a real passion for the game, he's got ability, and there's tremendous potential for growth."

The story went on to quote Leo Papile, about how I'd finally gotten my life together after struggling with issues familiar to kids with urban backgrounds. It quoted Heather saying how great it was for us to be back home, especially with the baby, and how proud she was of me. It quoted my mother saying how in one of the games I had been dribbling out the clock and I had been smiling.

"To me, it was the best part of the whole night," she said, "because I haven't seen Chris smile a lot with basketball in the last few years. I knew at that moment he had finally found a place where he likes to be, where he wants to stay. I think, finally, for the first time, Chris is at peace with himself."

If only that had been true.

It should have been, no question about that.

That was the year Heather and I handed out holiday turkeys in Fall River in conjunction with the Salvation Army. We did it for three years, buying a hundred turkeys the first year and three hundred by the third. It was my way of giving back, something that had been ingrained in me.

I remember being with my father when I was just a little kid, maybe eight years old, and we saw a kid playing basketball by himself with an old hoop on a telephone pole. My dad drove to the Gob Shop in Fall River and bought a backboard and a basket and brought it back to the kid. My father was always doing things like that for kids. He had grown up dirt poor, and he never forgot what it was like. He had a very big social conscience. My mother did, too. She used to give out dollar bills to kids in the Columbus Park Little League, many of whom were poor. She sometimes would take Michael and me to help out in a soup kitchen. I grew up with that. I grew up knowing that I should give back.

I always did free clinics at the Boys and Girls Club, and donated fifty tickets that year to Celtics games.

Michael was like that, too.

For years he ran a basketball league in the Harbor Terrace projects without getting any payment for it, spending countless hours there.

This is the way we were raised.

I loved to hang out at the Boys and Girls Club, shooting around with the kids, playing in the game room with them, Ping-Pong, pool, foosball. Kids loved kicking my ass. My picture in my Fresno State uniform was mounted in the wall. On the night they came to a Celtics game they had a big banner: FALL RIVER'S OWN: CHRIS HERREN. FROM THE BOYS AND GIRLS CLUB OF FALL RIVER.

In so many ways I had my childhood dream in the palm of my hand: playing for the Celtics in the shadow of my hometown.

And how many people ever get that?

I also had my dirty little secret.

And I was about to enter the gates of hell.

We practiced in the morning, and half an hour later I was on the road back to Fall River, less than an hour away if I hustled, to meet one of my dealers. Sometimes we'd meet at the Burger King on Route 24, sometimes in Fall River. Then I'd have to hustle home to where Heather and I were living in an apartment in Waltham, which was off Route 128, close to HealthPoint, the Celtics practice facility. I'd tell her that I'd stayed after practice working on my game.

But I rarely ever worked on basketball. Often, I was the last one to practice, and the first one to leave. Other guys would stick around, work on their game, maybe take more free throws, something. Not me. I was too busy working on my real game, which was making sure I had enough OxyContin to get through the day. That's what it was really about.

The irony was I did great at training camp, which I think surprised Pitino. As long as I had the drugs, I could play. I was still in the beginning of my addiction, and I could get away with it. After one preseason game he said in the papers that we hadn't run offense that well since he'd been in Boston, and during one preseason game after I made a couple of good passes, Tommy Heinsohn, the former Celtics great and longtime color man, said that he hadn't seen passes like that from a point guard since the legendary Bob Cousy. In one of the first games of the season I had fourteen points and nine assists and held the ball as the clock wound down in the Fleet Center. The next day I was on the back page of the *Boston Herald* with my fist thrown high in the air. One night after a game, Ted Sarandis, the host of a radio show on WEEI, said that the Celtics had found their point guard of the future. Dan Shaughnessy wrote a column in the *Boston Globe* saying that homeboy Matt Damon should come back and do the Chris Herren story.

There was talk of extending my contract, since I was on a one-year contract, and longtime Celtics broadcaster Mike Gorman had gone to Richard Pond, the money man for the Celtics.

"Do you know what you have here?" he said to Pond. "You have a white, local kid with charisma who has a shamrock tattooed on his arm."

It was all heady stuff, but I couldn't enjoy it. None of it mattered by then. My life was much too painful. Everything was about trying to get through the day and keep the lie going.

Playing underneath all those championship banners in the rafters?

Playing in the Fleet Center in the middle of downtown Boston?

Playing for the most storied basketball team in the world, the team I'd grown up idolizing?

It didn't mean anything.

I could have been sitting on a bench in Kansas for all I cared.

One day after practice Red Auerbach was in the next room holding court, talking about the old days, and I could have sat there and listened. How great would that have been? Instead, I had to hustle down Route 24 to meet some guy in a rest area so I could get through the next week. That was what was on my mind. Nothing else. Everything else went past me.

I had drug dealers FedExing packages to five-star hotels on the road. I was always making the ride down Route 24, speeding down, then speeding back, because I had to explain lost time to Heather.

Then my right shoulder started killing me. It was the day after we had played the Lakers in the Fleet Center, and I couldn't lift my right shoulder—not good when you're a right-handed player. After about a week, when it was apparent I couldn't play with it, surgery was scheduled at New England Baptist Hospital in Boston to repair a torn rotator cuff.

Then an interesting thing happened.

At the hospital they gave me anesthesia before the surgery and I didn't respond to it; it didn't knock me out.

The doctors couldn't figure it out.

"Is there any reason why he's not responding to anesthesia?" one of the doctors asked Heather.

"Not that I'm aware of," she said.

I could have told them.

That surgery was in December, and afterward they gave me a ton of OxyContin.

And when I came back to the Celtics two months later, everything had changed.

Pitino was gone, having resigned after a road game in Miami in late December, and Jim O'Brien had become the interim coach. Not the Jim O'Brien who had recruited me at Boston College. This Jim O'Brien had been one of Pitino's assistants both at the Knicks and at Kentucky.

A coaching change in midseason is always chaotic by definition. It's a seismic shift in a team. Pitino had not only been the coach, he had been the ultimate boss. Everything went through him. He made all the decisions. And now he was gone, leaving behind the uncertainty that came with his departure. It was like starting from scratch, every man for himself.

We never really clicked, O'Brien and I. It seemed like every time I'd come off a hotel elevator with a twelve-pack under my arm, he'd be standing there. I think he sensed something was off, something was wrong. I'm sure he thought I had a drinking problem. And all the momentum I'd built before the surgery was gone. I hadn't played in a while, the season had gone on without me, and that's another dirty little secret of the NBA: get hurt and it all goes on without you, a train that's left the station. Plus, my habit was getting worse. I was walking around with 1,200 milligrams of junk in my body every day. In O'Brien's defense, he had to win some games, convince management that he should be the coach. He was fighting for his coaching life, whether to get rehired by the Celtics or to show enough to get hired by someone else. He was on an NBA audition, with no safety net underneath him, because he was viewed as Pitino's guy and now Pitino was out of the league. O'Brien had his own things to worry about, as did all his assistants and the people around him. They had kids, bills to pay, real life issues, futures that could be up in the air if O'Brien couldn't convince management that he should be the full-time coach, not just the interim one. Dealing with Chris Herren was way down on his list.

The NBA is funny. You don't really have relationships with coaches, not the way you had in college. If you're helping someone climb the ladder, helping him survive, you're an ally. If you're not helping him, who cares? There's not a lot of sentiment one way or the other.

Then I missed a flight to the West Coast, the ultimate NBA sin. I was in such a fog I'd had the wrong day.

After that O'Brien had no faith in me, nor should he have.

And all the while my habit was getting worse.

Some nights on the road I was so depressed I would sit in my hotel room and cry, just lie there sobbing. I had become so strapped by my addiction. It had robbed me of so much. Many times coming clean and admitting everything was on the tip of my tongue, but I couldn't get the words out. The idea of the publicity, the shame, the horror of it, crippled me. There you are, sitting in the Four Seasons somewhere, about to play a game and then fly to some other city and some other five-star hotel, and what are you going to do, go knock on the coach's door and say you have to go to rehab? Knowing that as soon as you do that, the checks stop and your world crumbles, and nothing will ever be the same again?

Instead, you fight it.

You give yourself every pep talk you ever heard, all those ones about when the going gets tough the tough get going, all those slogans on locker room walls you grew up with, and you fight it.

You fight it and tell yourself that you need the drugs to make it through the season, but that when the season mercifully ends you will finally get yourself cleaned up and deal with this, because not to is like living inside the gates of hell.

One night I was in the players' parking lot at the Fleet Center in my Celtics warm-ups about a half hour before a game, waiting for one of my dealers to come up from Fall River, because if I didn't get my stuff I was too sick to even go through the pregame layup line, never mind actually play in the game. That was the reality of my life. I was at the mercy of drug dealers. If they weren't there when they were supposed to be, I couldn't function. Luckily, he arrived that night and I could play.

Another night I was at the back door in my warm-ups, waiting for another guy for the same thing.

That's what it had come down to.

Standing in the parking lot in my Celtics warm-ups waiting for a drug dealer.

And it was a long, long way from being that little kid in my

driveway playing imaginary games for the Celtics while pre-
tending I was Danny Ainge or Larry Bird, back when even the
thought of one day playing for the Celtics was the biggest dream
in the world.

■CHAPTER TEN■

Istanbul, Turkey, is beautiful, a fast-paced cosmopolitan city on the Bosphorus Strait, the only city in the world that is on two continents, the European and the Asian. It is the fourth largest city in the world, with a population of nearly 13 million, and has a history that dates back to something like 660 B.C. You can see the history everywhere, and even if you didn't know the specifics, you know you aren't in Kansas anymore.

But none of that mattered.

My father and I were in a hotel room while I was detoxing myself, trying to get better so I could play for a team that I had a contract with.

I needed the money, because things were sinking.

It was January 2002.

Five months earlier Heather and I had gone to Italy, where the plan was for me to play for a team in Bologna for $50,000 a month. The Celtics had made no offer to bring me back, and this was real money, a great opportunity. At least that's what my agents were telling me. Ex–NBA players are in demand in Europe, as basketball keeps getting bigger and bigger overseas, a worldwide game it hadn't been a generation ago, and on the surface this seemed great, certainly better than going into an NBA training camp without a contract. So Bologna had been on my radar for part of the summer. Frank Catapano talked about it a lot. How I could play there and make more money than I could make in the NBA.

There was only one problem.

I arrived in Bologna without any drugs, as the bag in which I had my pills hadn't arrived yet. When we landed, I was met by a guy from the team.

"Come on," he said. "You're going to practice."

So with Heather and Chris going off to a hotel, he hands me the keys to an Alfa Romeo. I jump in the car and start driving around Bologna for the next two hours in search of drugs.

But where?

I didn't speak any Italian, and I had no idea where I was going.

But I discovered something that would be true in all the places I went to play around the world. You want drugs? Go to the train station. Go to the bus station. You'll find drugs. Or they will find you.

I found this gypsy-looking dude at the train station. He didn't speak English. We were stuck in some bad scene from a bad movie. Yet drugs have become the universal language. He sold me a bag of heroin powder for $200, something to last a day or two, then gave me advice.

"Dark-skin men," he said in broken English. "Dark-skin men."

A couple of days later, the powder gone, I go back to the train station and find these two Nigerian-looking guys in their mid twenties who look a little shady. They look at me. I look at them. We go back and forth. Again, they don't speak English. Eventually, we work it out.

One of the guys had a string around his tooth. He unravels the string and starts to pull on it, and six little balloons of heroin come out of his stomach.

I thought it was a great sight.

Snorting the heroin was no different from taking OxyContin. It's the same junk, the same stuff. The misconception is that it's different, that somehow heroin is worse because the stigma is worse. It's not. It's the same.

The only difference?

When you start to snort heroin, you're one step closer to putting it in your arm.

At the time, Fortitudo Bologna was the biggest team in Europe, a team that played in the Euroleague, the elite league in Europe. The team was loaded with talent. The main guy was Gregore Fulka. He originally was from somewhere in the Balkans, but now lived in Italy. He was six eleven and could shoot both right-handed and left-handed from anywhere on the court, an amazing talent. He was in his thirties, and he was a huge star in Europe, one of those guys who everyone knew could play in the NBA, but who had such a sweetheart deal in Italy that he really didn't have to. There was another guy who eventually landed with the 76ers for a while, but I don't remember his name. The point is this was big-time basketball, and guys were pulling up in cars like they were in the NBA.

But the NBA spoils you.

I was the only American with Fortitudo, and right away that made it difficult. You have to immediately prove you're worth the money they're paying you. We probably had ten to fifteen practices, plus a couple of exhibition games, what they call "friendlys," and I could still play. My sickness was relatively new to me, and I had worked out over the summer, because that was part of my con. And even if my drug habit had become more important than my basketball, I knew I had to keep basketball going to keep the drugs going. In my twisted mind the two had become related; not only did basketball make me money, I also could hide behind it. As long as I was playing basketball, no one was looking at me too closely.

We first stayed in a tiny hotel room for a few days, then moved into an incredible apartment that had two floors and unbelievable paintings on the ceiling. But in the beginning there was one bed, one couch, old sheets, old blankets, a TV with only Italian stations. You realize that you're not in America anymore, that a lot of the things you took for granted are gone. None of us was happy. Christopher didn't have his toys. Heather went to check out the hospital where she was going to give birth in a couple of months and it all seemed so foreign to her. It was my first job overseas, and I didn't know if I could pull it off. For the first time I realized how spoiled I had been in the NBA.

Because the basketball in Europe is no bullshit. The players might not be as athletically gifted as they are in the NBA, but they are the same height as NBA players, and just as strong. They are all veterans, have been around. Then came the news that we were going to take a six-hour bus ride into the mountains to train for the upcoming season. This was something a lot of European teams did. Go away someplace and just train, as if they were marathon runners.

"Are you kidding me?" I said. "I'm going to ride a bus for six hours? This is a joke."

I was arrogant, had no clue.

It was early September, and I knew I was fucked. Where was I going to get any drugs in the middle of the mountains? And how was I going to survive two-a-day workouts if I was sick as a dog?

So here I am in some mountain town in Italy, with a maniac coach who wants us to run hills all day, and a six-foot-eleven guy from Bulgaria is my roommate, and I know that if I have to spend more time with this guy I'm probably going to kill him. There's no way in the world I can survive this. I'm dope sick and about to get worse.

"Fuck this shit," I said to the Bulgarian guy one night. "I can't take this anymore. I'm out of here."

"You're crazy, man," he said. "You'll never get a job like this again."

"I don't care. I'm going home."

But you know what?

He was exactly right.

I never got a job like that again.

Very soon after, September 11 happens. Heather's back in Bologna with little Chris and she's seven months pregnant with our second child. No one knows what's going to happen next, it's a scary time, and here we are on the other side of the world. And I'm about to be exposed. So I tell the coach I'm going back to the United States, that I can't stay in Italy anymore. It later got played up that it was because of 9/11, and there was even an Internet report that one of Heather's relatives had died in the World Trade Center, but that wasn't it. I was walking away from $50,000 a month because I was in the mountains in Italy and couldn't get any drugs.

Which, in some weird little slice of irony, got me into camp with the Celtics, because I returned before the NBA training camps opened. Frank Catapano worked out a deal to get me back with them, but without a guaranteed contact. Which meant that they could waive me at any time and it would cost them nothing.

Was I elated?

Was I thrilled?

Was I excited to once again be back with the Celtics?

None of the above.

I was numb.

So I'm in training camp with the Celtics, kind of going through the motions, my head somewhere else, someplace that had little to do with trying to make an NBA team. My addiction is getting worse, and the worse it gets, the more dependent I am on OxyContin. On the day before the real season started, just minutes away from getting on the bus at HealthPoint in Waltham to go to the airport to go wherever we were going to start the season, I walked into where we practiced to get my stuff for the trip.

"I'm sorry, Chris," one of the Celtics officials told me, "but you've been waived. You've got to clean out your locker."

"Keep my stuff," I said, walking out. "You can have it."

Ultimately, I had been the victim of the realities of the NBA, in that the Celtics had drafted Joe Forte, a guard out of North Carolina, as one of their three first-round picks the previous June, thus he had a guaranteed contract while I did not. So it really didn't matter that the coaching staff was not particularly enthralled with Forte, while I had had some good moments the year before and two years' experience in the league. As a first-round pick, Forte had two years guaranteed, with an option for a third, and there was no way the Celtics were going to cut him and eat that contract. That's just NBA reality. When you're fighting for those last roster spots, your contract is key, and often more important than how you're playing.

But it wasn't like I was crying into my pillow because the Celtics had waived me. It was absolutely irrelevant to me. The Celtics were the last thing on my mind. I knew basketball was going to end. There weren't too many long basketball careers in the world of heroin. And I knew that the year before, I had been a professional basketball player for two hours a day, and a professional drug addict for the other twenty-two hours. That was the reality. My basketball had become fraudulent.

I had real-world problems.

You dig yourself a hole, and that's what you're in, a constant hole. And it keeps getting deeper. I had more important things to worry about than the Celtics, namely to get another job overseas, and, just as important, to keep Heather from finding out the state of our finances. The key thing was the Paine Webber account, which I'd been raiding for a while, sometimes to the tune of $15,000 a month, and if she ever saw it she'd freak, know that something was really wrong.

Every morning I'd go to a 7-11 convenience store that had an ATM, and take out $200 or $300.

There had been $85,000 in the account when I started tapping it. There was something called "hit receipt," that told you what your balance was. Most days I wouldn't hit that, was afraid to hit it. I didn't want to know, because it was always going down. To $65,000. Then to $45,000. I was making frequent withdrawals, and never putting anything in. In the beginning I conned myself: $45,000 is all right, because I'll be putting money back in soon. Oops, fuck, now it's $30,000. Oh shit, now it's $20,000, and what's Heather going to do when she finds out? And now it's the fall and I don't have a job, rosters have filled up overseas, Heather's about to give birth, and what am I going to do?

So every day my game was to find the mailman before he came to the house. I would drive around the neighborhood looking for him, anything to keep that Paine Webber statement from coming to the house. That was the most important part of the day. Find that mailman. Try to keep the lie going.

That went on for three months.

In November our daughter, Samantha, was born in Providence, so now I had two kids and a dwindling bank account.

But that wasn't the only news that fall, not by a long shot.

I had started shooting heroin.

I had started snorting it in Italy, but when you enter the world of heroin, there aren't too many snorters. It's usually just a matter of time.

My time came one morning at a drug house in Fall River, as I was about to snort heroin. It was "below the hill," not too far from where my father had grown up, a tough neighborhood. It was a shithole. Four people were living there.

"Why don't you shoot it?" a woman said.

"I'm afraid of the needle."

She took my arm and stuck the needle in.

I went back to that house every morning for a month.

Shooting heroin was a totally different feeling, a totally different high. For one thing, it entered your bloodstream in three seconds, not the thirty seconds it took if you snorted it. The needle had so much power. It instantly took away the sickness, as if the needle had more power than the sickness. And I chased it. Chased the rush. Chased the high. There weren't very many hours I was straight.

But once you do the needle, you've crossed the line. It's a

scary day. You know you're crossing over, but it's not like there's a lot of rational thought going on. You hate yourself. Every time you use you're taking a chance of killing yourself, but you do it anyway. What's more self-destructive than that?

I knew when I did it that it was going to be a tough street to come back from. But there had been a lot of buildup, years of it. I had told myself countless times that I would never shoot heroin, that I would never go there, never do that. In my own twisted logic I had convinced myself that as long as I wasn't shooting it, I could stop anytime I really put my mind to it. Shooting it was the ultimate stigma, the ultimate taboo. I knew that there was a huge danger in having crossed that line.

And once you do, there's no more deceiving yourself. No more telling yourself that you can really quit anytime you want. No more deluding yourself into thinking that you have some control over your life. Now you've entered a dirty, dirty world. Now you're at the mercy of people who have no mercy.

You're a junkie.

So here my father and I were in this small room in an Istanbul hotel, and I'm trying to go cold turkey.

I had another contract that was going to start in a couple of weeks, and I had to get clean or there was no chance I'd be able to play. The first few days I told my father I had a stomach virus. That worked for a while. He didn't know about my addiction, because at that time no one knew. Then he started noticing vodka and whiskey bottles all over the place; I was using anything to get numb and knock myself out because I couldn't sleep.

"Chris, something's not right here," my father eventually said. "You're only sleeping ten minutes at a time, and your legs are kicking all over the place."

He knew the hell I was going through. He saw it. Before that he might have sensed something was up with me, and it probably was the reason he had volunteered to come get me settled in Turkey before Heather and the kids were scheduled to come. Now he knew.

"This is what this is, Chris?" he said. "Really?"

But my father had been around the block too many times to be totally shocked. He had seen guys he had grown up with buried because of drugs and alcohol. He also felt guilt about my addiction issues because of his drinking. That had come out in the family therapy sessions we'd had in Utah, and he had said in the documentary two years earlier that maybe things would have been different for me if our house hadn't been as volatile and competitive. So there was no anger from him over this, just concern.

"We'll get through this," he said.

Then the phone rang.

It was Heather back in Fall River.

She's not saying anything, just crying.

The Paine Webber statement had come in.

And in the house with her were her mother and my mother.

The jig was up.

But I was still sick. I'd been in Turkey a couple of weeks detoxing myself and starting to feel better, but I was still sick and there was a bellboy in his mid twenties who spoke a little English. I started working this kid, even through the language barrier. One day he brought me some marijuana.

I looked at it and shook my head.

His eyes got a little wide.

The next day he came back with hashish.

"No," I said.

His eyes got wider.

Then he came back with cocaine.

"No cocaine," I said, shaking my head.

Now his eyes were so wide they were buggin' out of his head. He pointed to his arm.

"Yes," I said, nodding.

Soon I was back to snorting heroin and my habit was back.

By this point we were living in a beautiful condo that looked out over the Adriatic. My father had gone back to Fall River. Heather, little Chris, and Samantha, who was three months old, were there. And I was back on the chase.

The team was called Galatasaray, and it had a huge tradition in Istanbul. They had kid teams, all kinds of teams, their own practice gym. There were sixteen teams in the league, and twelve were in Istanbul. We played in an arena that sat twelve thousand, and the fans were out of control. In the playoffs that year we played our big rival, Fenerbahce, a rivalry tied to soccer that had been going on for decades. We were in the third game of a best-of-five series and the crowd was nuts. Lighting off firecrackers inside the arena. Sending up flares. There were explosions all over the place. Before the game we had come out onto the court through a tunnel of police who were in riot gear.

The fans would heat coins with matches and throw them at you, try to burn you with them. There was a big Turkish center on our team and I was on a fast break with him and all of a sudden his neck snapped back. Someone had thrown a faucet at him, hit him in the forehead, and split his head open.

There were two other Americans on the team, and since I was a guard, that usually meant the other players were going to be big. The American players overseas were in two camps: older guys who were fading away, and guys who were two or three inches too short for their position in the NBA. That was the reality, and you first become aware of it in the predraft camp in Chicago, where you are measured and weighed. A lot of those six-foot-eight listings in college become six-foot-six, and that makes all the difference. NBA scouts never look at those players in the same way again. But there was still money to be made overseas, no question about it. I was making roughly $20,000 a month, real money in any league.

The coach knew I was fucked up. He didn't know how fucked up, and he didn't know on what, but he certainly knew something was off. Then again, my drug history in college was all over the Internet back then; Google me and it would come right up. He was a good guy, though; he understood me. He spoke English well, was in his early forties, and was a sort of Turkish playboy, and we got along well.

Because I could still play.

That's what it was all about.

If you could play, they would put up with just about anything. If you couldn't, they wanted nothing to do with you.

Istanbul was fast-paced, sexy, with water running through it, and blue mosques. Very cosmopolitan. You'd go to nightclubs there and it was like being in any big city in the world. There were also cops walking around with Uzis, and barefoot kids begging in the street. Every couple of hours sirens would go off, calling people to the mosques. And twenty miles away it was like Baghdad. Poor. Dusty. Concrete buildings. Cement everywhere.

I'd be standing around taxicab stands, everyone looking at me like I was up to no good. The drivers would take me miles away, to places where there were no foreigners, where the squalor was all around, the poverty overpowering. I'd have $500 to $1,000 in my pocket and I'd be by myself in places where I shouldn't have been alone. All I could think of was the movie *Midnight Express,* where the American kid goes to jail for drugs in Turkey and they throw away the key. Yet, ultimately, that still wasn't enough to stop me. The thought of going to jail didn't stop me. The thought of losing everything I loved in the world didn't stop me. Nothing stopped me. In the end it didn't matter what country I was in. I could have been on any block in any country in the world. I was a country all by myself.

I was on my way down.

And I was willing to risk everything.

■CHAPTER ELEVEN■

I wasn't trying to get back to the NBA then, even though a lot of the people around me were talking about that, and even though I had been the last cut by the Celtics the year before. I knew who I was. Even if I'd come home for the summer, to Fall River, and talked a good game and acted like that was the goal, I knew that being fucked up all the time wasn't exactly conducive to getting back to the NBA.

I just wanted another paycheck.

I was still a professional basketball player.

That's all I knew.

Where else was I going to get the kind of money to support both a family and a $500-a-day drug habit?

So I still worked out at the Boys Club in Fall River, though usually not for very long or very hard. I still kept up the appearance of someone who was serious about his career, someone who was married with two small children and owned a small house on Bond Street in Fall River, in the same neighborhood I had grown up in and across the street from my father, who had remarried. My mother was living in Portsmouth, Rhode Island, about fifteen minutes away. Michael was in Fall River, doing a sports talk show on a local radio station, where he was called "The Hurricane." If you didn't know any better, and didn't look too closely, you would have thought I was doing fine, not in the NBA, but playing overseas for big money.

My nightmare hadn't gone public.

My family knew.

A few people close to me knew.

They didn't know the specifics, and they certainly didn't know the extent of my addiction. They knew that something wasn't right, though.

But it's easy to fool people when you have money in your pocket and you have a place to live. It's easy to fool people when your family is with you and everything looks fine.

And I was adept at running away from people. My ADD became useful. If I hadn't been comfortable in my own skin before, how do you think I was when someone wanted to sit me down and talk about my problems?

My mother was always saying she was praying for me, but she had grown up with alcoholics in her family, so this wasn't a totally foreign world to her.

It was to Heather, though, and she was heartbroken. She also was angry and felt betrayed.

So I would lie to her, say it was better, that I had it under control.

I kept living that lie, and felt more and more guilty every time I told it.

And how did I deal with the guilt?

I got high.

Then came a job in Beijing.

But China was tough.

Basketball overseas is difficult, even for someone who is healthy. There is tremendous pressure on the American players. Start with the fact that the other players resent you, because usually you're making more money than they are. Then the coach is under the gun, so you better show him that you can help him win, or he's going to turn on you. They want to see how good you are right away. There's no time to play yourself into shape, no time to settle in to your surroundings. You've got to go right off the jump.

Then there's the language barrier, which makes all conversations blunt.

"You play suck."

"You no good."

"We send you home."

These teams always had other foreign players on the back burner, guys they were waiting to bring in if they didn't like you. That was the unwritten deal: play well, or they would send you home.

There were other realities about playing basketball overseas, too. You had no chance of getting your last paycheck, because what were you going to do if you didn't get it? Stay around and wait for it? Sue them?

So I would have felt pressure even if I had been healthy.

The team was called Shougang Beijing Ducks, and it was in the Chinese Basketball Association. Basketball is very popular in China. People love it. Every arena was full. The games were on television. There was a lot of media attention, constant interviews, and there were NBA signs everywhere. There were billboards with Yao Ming, who had just gone to the United States, and other Chinese stars on them. Some of our games were a three-hour plane ride away. Basketball had been around since the early years of the twentieth century when American missionaries first brought the game to China, and the story was that basketball had survived the Cultural Revolution because Mao liked it.

Basketball in Beijing was special, and my team did it right. They were sponsored by Nike, and they had a lot of resources. They did everything in their power to make me feel comfortable, everything they could to make it an easy adjustment. They made sure I was taken care of.

We had a huge following. We played in a beautiful arena that sat twelve thousand, and we often got crowds of ten thousand. We had a brand-new weight room. We had catered lunches at practice, rooms to take naps in. There were dancers. There were cheerleaders. There were halftime shows. The whole thing was a spectacle. There was nothing minor league about it. It was a professional team in every sense of the word. It had a real NBA feel to it.

There were only two non-Chinese players on the roster, a seven-foot-two center named Garth Joseph, who had played college basketball in the States, and me. In the beginning I hadn't been there long enough to find drugs, so I was sick, and for three and a half weeks it was sheer hell. Try being in a taxicab and you're sweating bullets and you're also freezing, and maybe you're throwing up, and maybe you have diarrhea, and you're on your way to run up and down a basketball court for two and a half hours. Try playing basketball when what you really want to be doing is lying down in the fetal position somewhere, moaning.

Beijing was intimidating, with millions and millions of people. Downtown Beijing is like Times Square, bright, fast-paced, with every brand-name store you can name. There is incredible traffic, to the point that where we were practicing was only fifteen miles away, but sometimes it would take an hour to get there. I would take a cab every day, and every day we would go a different route, and every day there would be a different fare. The cab drivers were always hustling me. There was smog everywhere. One night one of my taxi drivers invited me over for dinner and the ceilings were six feet high in the front room and four feet high in the bedrooms. It was so very different. Yet there were a lot of foreigners in Beijing, and the French, German, and English embassies were only a couple of blocks away from the apartment where we lived. The apartment building had both a fitness club and a supermarket.

Beijing was all about extremes, one block upper-class, the next Third World. It was a city on the go, no question about that. Constant movement. Beijing was getting ready for the Olympics, and there was building everywhere. Yet there were unbelievable contrasts, too. People chopping chickens' heads off on street corners. Animals bleeding out in the street. Poverty that Americans have no idea about.

One night I'm in this nightclub that has a real international flavor, called the Shark Bar, with several foreign players. In a sense all the clubs overseas were the same: dark, loud music, a sense of unreality, their own world. We're all drinking, and because I'm drinking, the cocaine comes calling. One thing leads to another and I get some white powder. But it wasn't coke. It was heroin, what's called China White.

Back again.

That's when my new best friend entered my life.

He was Nigerian, and he could get China White.

So wherever I went, he was nearby. I bought every day. I still have a picture of all of us sightseeing in Beijing.

Heather.

The kids.

My drug dealer.

The perfect little family.

The irony was, I could play basketball on heroin. I even had sixty-something points in a game one day, a Chinese Basketball

Association record for a foreign player. It still might be, for all I know. But I was out of control. I had money, which allowed me to keep feeding my habit. I had time. I had opportunity, and I always did things in extremes. I never went at anything easy. I had become a society junkie, someone who could hide his addiction because I had money.

Heather was starting to find things around the apartment, empty little packets. She knew. But what was she going to do about it, except yell and cry and ask me what I was doing to myself? She was a long way from home with two small kids and a husband with a serious problem. She was extremely hurt and angry. She would yell at me, but I would yell louder. That was my tactic. I had come out of a family where whoever yelled the loudest won the argument.

I yelled louder.

"Fuck you, Heather. You're crazy."

"You really need help, Heather. You're losing it."

"You're delusional, Heather, you really are."

This was my message every time I felt attacked. I would lash out, turn it around. I tormented my poor wife.

But you know what?

On heroin, I cooked the food. I vacuumed the apartment. I washed the clothes. I went to the store. I did anything she wanted me to do. Without it? I was irritable, angry, impossible to live with. Without it I wasn't making any beds, cooking any meals. Without it I wasn't doing anything. That was another insidious thing about it.

But I was borderline out of control, no question about that.

One day Heather was out shopping and then was going to the gym. I was babysitting. I was also secretly smoking hash, something I did a lot of that year, in addition to the heroin. Sammy was taking a nap, and Chris was playing a video game. We were living on the sixth floor.

I decide to take the trash downstairs.

"Don't close the door," I tell Chris. "I'll be right back."

I put the trash in the bin and start going up the stairs when I hear Chris yelling. He's standing at the top of the stairs, and the door to the apartment is closed.

"You closed the door," I say to Chris, "and your sister is in there sleeping."

I don't have the key, and I'm baked from the hash. So I call security, and two guys come up, but they don't speak English, they don't have a key, and I'm losing it. I can hear Sammy crying, Chris keeps saying he didn't close the door, and now I'm in a panic.

"Stand back!" I yell.

I back up, then take a couple of quick steps and kick the door, knocking it right off its hinges. The wood splinters, and there in front of me is a terrified Chinese couple sitting on their couch. And there on the door I've just destroyed is the number 53, while my apartment is number 63.

And there on the next floor was our open door, just as Christopher had said it was.

That little incident cost me $700 to fix the door.

I liked my coach. I liked my teammates. We would go out together on the road and we would sit in bars. I had learned to say hello and good-bye in Chinese, basic things like "How are you?" and "Thank you," but that was about it. My teammates didn't know much English. But somehow we communicated, and somehow it worked. I ate dog, turtle, crickets, all kinds of fish. But that was on the road. At home it wasn't like I was living in that strange of a world. I was playing basketball. My family was there. I had American TV; I had American food.

And I had drug dealers on call.

That's like living in Fall River.

But if you had taken away my drug dealers I would have been fucked.

The season continued, another one of those lost years, me using the junk as maintenance, to get through the day, go to practice, play in the games, just keep going. I didn't care how I played. Basketball was irrelevant. The road trips could be torture because I'd run out of drugs, and by the time they were over I could have been on the Gaza Strip for all I cared. And my body was starting to break down.

Once we played in a town on the Pakistan border where guys were walking around with knives that looked like swords stuck in the waistbands of their pants. It was cold, gray, smog near the ground. They didn't even look Chinese; they were more Mongolian looking. We went from the hotel room to the restaurant, back to the room. I was told not to leave the hotel because they didn't like Americans around there, and there were stories of people getting kidnapped. Near the end of the season the SARS epidemic exploded in China. It began in Guangdong Province, where we played the semifinals of the Chinese Basketball Association, the game that ended our season.

Shortly after that, I left.

But not before stiffing some Nigerian drug dealers for $6,000.

I told them I was leaving the next week and left the next day.

No honor among thieves.

When I went back to China the next year, I went alone.

Before I went, though, I went to a Massachusetts doctor. For $500 in cash he was going to put a pellet under my skin that was going to be an opiate blocker. Heather and I went together, but while she was outside in the waiting room I took a razor blade and cut my skin, put a patch over it, and pocketed the $500, which I later used to buy pills. Heather never knew.

This time it wasn't Beijing and a lot of money. This time it was somewhere called Nanjing for less money.

But it was a job and I had no choice. Or so I thought.

I landed in Shanghai, which is another jumpin' place, looks like a mini New York. I landed loaded.

"How far is Nanjing?" I asked my translator, who had met me at the airport.

"Three and a half hours," he said.

Nanjing was in the middle of nowhere. I stayed in one of the suburbs where there always seemed to be smog and the smell of burning trash. It was incredibly ugly, cement everywhere. There were few cars, and the taxis were these little things with three wheels. There were people in the street cutting the heads off of chickens and selling them. There were little kids collecting broken glass in the street to sell to factories. There were no Americans anywhere. The hotel was terrible. The TV only had nine channels. One was in English, but it was full of Chinese shows. It was a miserable, miserable place, and I hated every minute of it. I would sit in my hotel room and drink and wait to pass out.

After three weeks the pills were gone and I couldn't get any more. It was the first time I hadn't been able to get drugs overseas. Now I was starting to get sick.

The place is horrible, and I'm horrible, and I'm supposed to spend a season here?

And now I'm trying to kick heroin.

Trust me, I wasn't going to find any heroin in this town.

There was a better chance of hell freezing over than there was of me finding opiates in this town. No bus terminal. No train station. Nothing. It was one big industrial-looking place full of people who all looked the same. There was no way I could hit the streets there.

So I started drinking vodka, and very soon I was doing it heavy. Drinking every day, trying to get numb. I would sleep for something like two hours a night, then have to get up at nine in the morning sick as a dog and go to practice all stressed out.

Would they send me home?

And then what?

So I would get more booze and try to tough it out.

We would take these nine-hour bus rides and I'd drink for seven of them. Then I'd black out. The team must have thought I was crazy. They had to. I couldn't wait for it to end, but it ended sooner than I thought.

One night we were in a club, several of us from the team. It was on the road somewhere, I don't even remember where. It was a bar full of foreigners. I was drinking, and when I drank I became aggressive, and I got into a beef with a Japanese kid who spit in my face. So I sucker punched him. The kid began to fall. I kept hitting him. Then I hit his friend, who was running at me. But he was a bouncer and I could see the sheer look of panic on the faces of the people I was with. There were four hundred people in the room, and all of a sudden the music stops. My friends are trying to get me out the back door. But eight guys are standing there. The lights are on by now, and there are guys with machetes.

Then the cops dragged me off to jail. They put me in a cell. I was probably in there for four hours, and I could hear the guards talking, but I couldn't understand them. It cost me a couple of grand to get out, and after that the team sent me home.

Then it was three weeks in Poland, in Warsaw.

Different country, same script.

It's bleak and cold, and I'm miserable, sitting in some hotel room drinking by myself, unable to sleep, praying I'll fall asleep, finally grabbing a few hours, then getting up in the morning and trying to play basketball, until they sent me home.

I took my issues back home with me, of course.

The summer before I went to Nanjing I had gone to a hospital in Worcester, Massachusetts, a three-week rehab arranged by Mikey Martin. When I came out I was supposed to go to twelve-step meetings, but that didn't last, and before you knew it I was back to the chase again. It was getting old, not only for me, but for Heather, too.

That summer we were living with Heather's parents in Newport, Rhode Island, having sold the house in Fall River because it was now too small with two kids. Her parents had a town house right off Bellevue Avenue, once the address of some of the richest people in America, a beautiful street full of mansions. This was the Newport of legend. At one end of the street was the Tennis Hall of Fame, and at the other was Ocean Drive, where the tourists went.

It was an incredible place to be living, but it was all lost on me.

I was too far into the nightmare.

It was getting more and more difficult to go overseas, but what else to do? Try to be an assistant coach at a college somewhere? I didn't have my degree. Try to take over Heather's father's office supply store in Fall River, where I worked one summer and liked it? Go back to school somewhere and finish my degree? Try to find a normal life, whatever that was?

I had all sorts of good intentions, wanted in so many ways to get off this carousel I was on. But then I would go use again and it just kept going round and round. One night Heather's sister says a friend of hers saw me at a drug dealer's house in Newport, Heather goes crazy, and I spend a few nights in one of the low-rent motels by the beach. But to be away from the kids was its own kind of torture, so I would beg and promise and she'd take me back.

Why did she take me back after all this?

She took me back because she still believed in me, and because I was always telling her I could get through this. I was selling hope, not only to her, but to myself, too. I didn't want to keep living like this. I knew how destructive it was. I saw what it was doing to Heather: beating her down, putting her in the middle between me and her family. I knew the ramifications for the kids. I knew these things. So there were a million times I'd tell myself that I had to stop this, that it was insanity.

I always believed I could stop, always believed that if I could just get through this hell, that would be it, no more. And after Beijing, Heather hadn't been overseas with me, hadn't been in Nanjing and Warsaw, and when I wasn't around, things stabilized for her. The drama in the house wasn't there. I was sending money home. And deep down Heather truly wanted to believe that things were getting better, that somehow I was going to get through this and we could start living a normal life.

Then I'd come home and all the drama would start up again.

And all the while there are the plans for the next year, one more basketball payday where we all can go and be a family, not some hellhole like Nanjing, China, because there's still the NBA on the résumé and that still has cachet, and maybe I can get one more chance to come out of this tailspin and make everything right again. That's what's going on in my head, this fantasy that somehow I can turn this around and make everything right again. There were opportunities in both Germany and France, for maybe $9,000, $10,000 a month, and if I wasn't so fucked up that would have been good money in good countries, an easy life. But in my twisted mind that wasn't enough money; we needed another big payday because all the accounts were going down. I'd end up screaming at both Frank and Mikey, telling them I needed more money, they had to find me a job with more money.

"What the fuck, Frank? I played in the NBA, and you can't get me a job? What am I supposed to do?"

He eventually got me a spot on the Dallas Mavericks summer league team.

I went to Dallas for a week or so to practice, but once again it became the same old story. One night I went out with a teammate and ended up at a block party in the ghetto and there were cops everywhere and me wandering around with my shirt off, completely fucked up.

The summer league was hosted by the Celtics. It was held at UMass-Boston, the same gym in which I had ended two seasons at Durfee. So, in a sense, it was a homecoming. In the first game I had a great game, played so well that guys from NBA teams were coming up to Frank afterward.

"What's up with Herren? Where's he been?"

If they only knew.

Danny Ainge, the former Celtic who was now the boss of the Celtics, was in the first row. So was Larry Bird. So were many people in the NBA.

I had another good game the next afternoon, and there were stories in both the *Globe* and the *Herald* about my overseas odyssey, my return to Boston, and how I had played myself back onto the NBA radar screen.

Then I tweaked my knee, it blew up, and that was it for the summer league.

We were living in my mother's house in Portsmouth, Rhode Island, then. It was a split-level in a great neighborhood between East and West Main roads, the two roads that run through Aquidneck Island. It was quiet and peaceful. Some of the houses had baskets in the driveway. Little kids would ride their bikes in the street. Our kids had playmates, and Heather had made friends with some people in the neighborhood. From the outside it all seemed normal. Inside, I was still a junkie, however much I tried to hide and maintain the illusion that everything was fine. I was still all about the con.

And now every day became a grind.

How were we going to get money?

How were we going to live?

What if I couldn't get another gig overseas?

How could I keep this fragile little house of cards together?

If it had been just me, I would have run and hid, just taken off and gone somewhere else, anywhere else. That was the fantasy all those nights when I couldn't sleep and my mind was racing and my feet were twitching, and my body felt like it was never going to be able to slow down. But it wasn't just me. It was Heather and the kids. And it was the guilt. The incredible guilt. I looked at Heather, this poor woman who had picked me, had picked me to share her life with, had picked me to be the father of her children, and it broke my heart. But I was powerless to do anything about it. Eventually, I told everyone that I wasn't going overseas, that I was going to the Continental Basketball Association with the hope of getting back to the NBA. I told everyone that my showing in the summer league had me back on the NBA's radar, and rather than go overseas again, out of sight and out of mind, I would be in the CBA, just ready to be called up to the NBA. I was trying to give hope.

To Heather.

To my family.

To everyone.

But I was hopeless.

I ended up in Bismarck, North Dakota, about as far off the radar as you can get. I lived in a small motel room. I was making very little money, and felt like I had woken up on the far side of Mars.

When I realized I couldn't easily get drugs there, I'd periodically fly back to Providence, Rhode Island, to buy them on the street, then turn around and quickly fly back. No one knew. Not even Heather. I'd just fly in from North Dakota, turn around, and fly back. I probably did that four times. Bismarck to Chicago, Chicago to Providence.

In early December 2004, while I was home for a few days, it all came crashing down on me.

All the lies.

All the cons.

All the betrayals.

The whole show ended because of what, on the surface, seemed the most innocent of things.

Unless, of course, you've just shot heroin and you're completely fucked up.

The plan was to go to the Dunkin' Donuts and buy some doughnuts and stuff for the kids.

Until I passed out in the car a few hundred yards from my house, and only a couple of hundred yards from where little Chris went to school.

It was about eight in the morning.

"Herren remained unconscious for the next several minutes, forcing police and rescue officials to break the rear driver's side window to remove the former Boston Celtics shooting guard," one newspaper reported. "Herren, police said, was revived by medical rescue and was transported to Newport Hospital, where he was treated and released."

But I hadn't been released.

After I was removed from the car, police found drug paraphernalia and eighteen empty packets of heroin in the car, and they arrested me at Newport Hospital. They took me back to the police station, where I was in a cell most of the day before being officially charged that night by a justice of the peace and released on bail.

"This is my career," I was quoted as saying. "This is my life. I am very worried about the whole thing. This is just crazy."

Crazy, indeed.

■CHAPTER TWELVE■

It was all public now, as public as the newspaper and the local TV news.

This wasn't college. There, as embarrassing as my cocaine problems were when they were publicly revealed, they could be dismissed as youthful mistakes. I was a screwed-up kid who had gotten in trouble with cocaine but had been to rehab and seen the error of his ways and learned from the experience. That had been the perception, one buffeted by countless newspaper stories and my playing in the NBA for two years.

Few people had known about my addiction.

No one knew about the problems overseas.

I was still someone who was getting good money to play basketball.

I was still the six-foot-two white kid from Fall River who had made it all the way to the NBA, who still was, on the surface anyway, a great story.

Now all of that had been shattered.

I wasn't just a junkie.

I was a public junkie.

Complete with the overpowering shame that came with that.

I couldn't look people in the eye. It was like my head weighed fifty pounds, like I couldn't raise it. I basically stayed in the house, became a recluse. I focused on being the best parent I could be, always at home, always trying to do things with the kids. I only left my house to go to Fall River and buy drugs on the sneak. I didn't care what I looked like. I didn't care what clothes I wore. Every day I wore the same things: jeans, a shirt, a pair of boots.

I wouldn't go to Marzilli's, the grinder shop on Bedford Street in Fall River where I used to go all the time.

I wouldn't go to Durfee games.

I wouldn't go anywhere.

Shame is a horrible thing.

But do you know what real shame is?

When you no longer have any shame.

I wasn't there yet.

I was in the court system, though. There were appearances. There were lawyers' fees. There were more court appearances. There were more lawyers' fees. There was the constant shame of having to be in court in Newport, standing in front of a judge, knowing that everyone knew who I was, people nodding over at me with their knowing looks, Chris Herren the drug addict.

This became my everyday baggage, a daily carousel of shame and guilt, regret and embarrassment.

And the worst part was that for all my legal problems, I still was an addict. That hadn't magically gone away when all this went public, or when I walked into the courthouse. I was still on the carousel. The one that went round and round and always came back to the same place. Every day. No progress was ever made. You end up living fifteen minutes at a time. One hustle to the next. Running out of money. Calling people, but nobody answers. Leaving messages and nobody calls you back.

No surprise.

I wouldn't have called me back either.

I went through my small pension for playing two years in the NBA.

I borrowed money from the few people left in the world who still felt sorry for me.

I got a job shoveling cement the next summer. It was at a place in East Providence, Rhode Island. It was one big gravel pit, with big piles of sand everywhere, and my job basically was to shovel it. Much of the time I was the only person doing this, just me and these dunes of gravel, as the couple of guys who ran the place would sit in the small trailer that was the office. Many days it would be blistering hot, and I would be there shoveling, either on something or sick because I was not, and thinking that here was where the devil really lived.

It was a long way from the NBA.

Real life was becoming a real issue. The lack of money. The shit job. The disintegrating marriage. The future that seemed to stop at fifteen minutes down the road. The self-hatred. The hope-lessness.

The only good news was that my kids seemed to be surviv-ing, and that was because of Heather and the Portsmouth school system. Everybody at the kids' school knew that Heather was rock solid. Everybody knew that she was all over the kids and their lives. She read to them every night. She helped them with their homework. They were well-behaved, did well in school. And Chris had an amazing teacher that year. She knew what was going on, took a special interest in him.

Somewhere in there my grandfather died, and that was an-other blow. Not only had he always given me unquestioning support, but he had always been a place I could go and get away from everything else. We would sit there together and eat his walnut ice cream and everything seemed more peaceful, not as important. Now he was gone.

Then my mother was diagnosed with cancer. My mother had always been there for me emotionally when I was a kid. In the family dynamic it had been my mother and me against my fa-ther and brother. They would call me a mama's boy when I was young and didn't want to play sports. She was the one who never pushed me, who said that if I had grown up in a different environment I'd probably never have played basketball. She was the one who went to the Durfee games and judged me not by how many points I scored, or by how I was playing, but by whether it looked as if I was having fun. She would even do that in the NBA. Nothing else mattered to her. She would go to Durfee games and look at all of us who had grown up together and want everyone to be happy. She was the one who thought that so much of it had become negative, the controversy that had surrounded Michael at Durfee, the furor that had surrounded me. She was the one who had said that basketball was a runaway locomotive in our family. That if she had had the power back then, she would have written a very different script.

She was always worrying about me, praying I could get my life turned around, devastated by my addiction but still believing in me, always that. She had been there in the house when Heather had called me in Istanbul, the day she had found out that the Paine Webber account was gone, the day they both became aware of my problem. I hid the extent of it from her, the way I hid it from everyone. I became very skilled at hiding it. But after that phone call she looked at me with love, but with pity, too.

"Christopher," she said to me one day, "I know what you're doing. I hired a private detective and I know what you're doing. You need help."

I ran from that. I was beyond help. I was beyond counselors and therapists.

And now she was dying too soon right in front of me, and my head was simply not there. I was in a fog. She was going downhill in a hurry, and near the end she was staying at my uncle Billy's house in nearby Swansea and I would go there and sit in the room with her and watch her sleep. There was no way I could deal with it emotionally; it was way beyond me.

I remember sitting in the church at her funeral mass.

"Chris, you're sweating," Michael said.

I didn't have an answer.

But Michael always knew what was going on with me. He could read me in ways others couldn't. That was one of the reasons I often ran from him.

She was buried on a blistering hot morning in August 2005 in St. Patrick's cemetery in Fall River, all of us standing there as her casket was lowered into the ground.

I was high on heroin.

There was another overseas basketball job, though.

"Where is it?" I asked Frank Catapano.

"Tehran," Catapano said.

"You're crazy."

When I landed I was quickly taken into a room where two guards went through everything I owned.

"You do it to our people when we come to the U.S.," one of them said, almost apologetically.

Welcome to Iran.

It was the fall of 2006, and this was the last stop on my basketball journey. This was what it had come down to, this place where few Americans ever go, in the "axis of evil." But I felt welcome there. I never felt any anxiety. I was never scared. I rode in taxicabs by myself. I went out at night. People there were fascinated by Americans, by the freedoms we had. They didn't like

George W. Bush, but they loved our freedoms. They were very, very open to me being an American. Tehran might have been the friendliest place I lived overseas.

"Chris, I thought they didn't like Americans in Iran," a friend said over the phone one day.

"They like me," I said.

But I was running out of time, and I really couldn't function. I was always sick, and because of that, training camp was brutal. And it wasn't just being sick. I had been sick for too long. I was terribly ill, emotionally. My spirit was gone. In the beginning I couldn't get heroin, and I didn't want that life anymore. But I didn't know how to live without drugs. I did a lot of coke, getting it from my taxi driver, and a lot of drinking, much of the alcohol smuggled in in bottles covered in dirt.

My driver was Iranian, but he spoke English. He would show up every morning outside my hotel with cocaine tied into a sock and throw it up to my second-floor balcony.

Once I had been there for a while I knew I could get heroin if I wanted it. It was there.

But I was trying to quit.

Opiates had caused so much misery in my life.

How many times had I bought a thousand dollars' worth of pills and told myself I'd take five that day and four the next and then three, and then one, and then there would be none left and that would be it? How many times had I bought the opiate blocker Suboxone, which makes you terribly sick if you put opiates into your system, only to still want to get high, even knowing how sick it was going to make me?

It seemed like I had been trying to quit forever.

But I was too far gone to quit.

I lived in the mountains. It was beautiful, with a lot of stucco buildings. There were ski slopes open. You didn't see the poverty there. The mountains were where the money was in Tehran. It got poorer as you went farther down into the city, and the architecture changed, more cement. Tehran was huge, overpowering. There were sprawling housing projects, and it was a little like New York, little cities within the larger city. My coach lived in one of them. It had four high-rises, each one maybe forty-stories high. He was Iranian, mid-fifties, a good guy, but the language gap was big and we couldn't communicate in a clear way. American music was banned in Tehran, even though it was always on the radio in the cabs. The drivers would blast it, sing along to the songs, knowing all the words. There was very little Internet. Alcohol was illegal, though it was easy to get. Tehran was foreign, but I had lived in different places by then, so I was used to it. People were people, wherever they were. Some good, some bad. But mostly good.

The hotel wasn't bad. It had twelve channels, and you could get CNN, ESPN, a lot of stuff. Iran is not as isolated as most Americans think it is, not as isolated as parts of China. We played about twenty minutes away. The gym was small; it held maybe three thousand. Women weren't allowed to go to most games, and when they were, they had to sit on one side of the gym and only in the upper levels. The crowd was mostly made up of teenaged and middle-aged men.

Basketball was not very big in Iran, nowhere near as big as it had been in the other places I'd been overseas. My team was called Paykan (it was sponsored by an Iranian automobile company of the same name), and to get to practice you had to walk through two security checkpoints, then through steam and part of the assembly line to get to the gym. The average crowd at games was just a few hundred people, but they were into it. And the Iranian players were in great shape. They had a six-foot-eleven guy, and other guys who were big and strong. And the money was good. There were guys I knew from Fresno who were playing overseas in Italy, Germany, and Switzerland for $4,000 a month, and I was making $12,000.

I was befriended by an older man, a big fan of the team, who ran a dry cleaning shop. My salary got funneled to me through his daughter in San Francisco who would wire it into my account. He spoke English, and we would sit and drink tea together.

I got to know a few people.

One man told me he prayed every night that the United States would invade his country and free all the people. I had dinner in several homes and talked to women who were not wearing their head scarves, which they had to wear in public. Just about everyone I met said how much they despised the government and how much they would like to live in America. They said that they wished the royal family were still there, that life in Iran had been better when the royal family was in power. These were middle-class people. Maybe it was different for others, but my experiences were positive.

The coach knew something was wrong with me, but had no time to deal with those kinds of things. After about a month it was time for me to go.

Back to the same world I had left four months earlier.

A friend threw me a life preserver.

Or at least she tried.

Her name is Mary Parker, and she was one of my communications teachers at Fresno State. Her granddaughter loved Fresno State basketball, and I had been a surprise guest at one of her birthday parties. Mary and her husband, Steve, who was an eye doctor, had come to my wedding in Fall River. Now she was inviting us all to come stay with her and her husband in their home in California. She was offering me another chance; to get away from Fall River, go back to California, and finish my degree in a place where a lot of people still had affection for me.

The Parkers lived in a beautiful home in Oakhurst, a town near the entrance to Yosemite National Park, in the mountains, less than an hour from Fresno. There was an apartment downstairs, and the plan was for me to go first, then Heather and the kids would follow when Chris got out of school.

The area was very rural—it was not uncommon to see

bears—and in a perfect world it would have been a great place to make a new start. No one there knew what had happened to me. It felt like a new beginning. There was a resort hotel in the neighborhood, and I made a few bucks as a fitness instructor. I was thinking maybe I could run a little basketball school there. But I was still constantly running, and this became just another spot to delay the inevitable.

There was no heroin, at least not in the beginning. Instead, I became a drunk. I would drink anything and everything, drink until I became numb. In many ways it was one of the worst times in my life, for everything was spinning out of control, regardless of the change in zip code.

Two months in I connected with a guy who had played football for Fresno State when I was there, and I was off and running with him. I started disappearing for days at a time, and the Parkers were getting both worried and frustrated. I still had no money. But when the guy went out, I went out, and it started getting ugly. His ex-wife had been a cheerleader at Fresno, and she warned me about him. I didn't listen. The power of drugs was too strong. I started staying with him for days at a time. I'd be up for five days hallucinating, paranoid. We were smoking crystal meth, which is the worst drug there is, far worse than heroin.

Then Heather and the kids were due in at the Oakland Airport, about two and a half hours away.

I rent a Cadillac Escalade, but I'm fucked up, and getting paranoid, and looking at the clock, and there's no way I'm going to get there in time, because now I'm lost in Modesto, which isn't even close to Oakland. I pull the car over to the breakdown lane and get out. I'm trying to get people to stop so I can ask them for help. Then I start running down the highway, but my legs give out and I'm on the highway when the police come. They put me in handcuffs, throw me in the back of a sedan, and take me to jail.

A couple of days later I get released. Outside the doors are the streets of Modesto. It's mid-afternoon, ninety degrees. I have no shoelaces, and a ripped shirt. There are four dollars in my pocket. I go into a 7-11 and buy a couple of beers, go behind the store to drink them, and fall asleep.

"Hey man, you alive?"

Two dudes, one white and one black, were poking me with their feet.

"You alive?"

We ended up drinking together for a few hours in back of the 7-11.

Eventually, someone came down from Fresno to get me. That was how I reunited with Heather and the kids.

Two weeks later, back in Oakhurst, that same Fresno football player called me.

"Let's go out," he said.

"No. I can't. Heather's here."

"Come on."

"Can't do it."

The next day I heard that he and his girlfriend had been shot and killed, in what was being called an execution.

A few months later Heather and the kids went back to Portsmouth. She simply couldn't deal with my drinking anymore. She went home to find her mother very sick with gastrointestinal cancer, an illness she would die of just months later. So now Heather had lost her mother, and the kids had lost their grandmother, with whom they had spent a lot of time and whom they adored. Her entire world had collapsed on her, and still Heather kept things together at home. And I was back in California using crystal meth.

It was getting ugly out there. The Parkers had done everything in their power to help me, but I was too far gone. I couldn't continue to torture them the way I was doing. That had become the story of my life, torturing people who were trying to help me, and then running from them.

When I came back, Heather and the kids were living with her father in the house in Portsmouth and I was out. I moved in with my aunt in Fall River, until my father found some drug paraphernalia and that was that. So he and I were battling. He was at his wit's end. He didn't know what to do. No one knew what to do. I had nowhere to go,

I ended up in a motel in Middletown, the town between Portsmouth and Newport. Heather dropped me off.

"All I want you to do, Chris, is be the person I married," she said. "You have to get yourself together, or we can't do this."

She wasn't angry. She was already on the far side of anger.

"You've got to get yourself together to be there for the kids," she said, before driving off.

What was left unsaid that day was that it might be too late for us, that she simply had been through too much. Who could have blamed her?

I remember lying there in that room and the agony of knowing that Heather and the kids were just a few miles away.

Soon after, she took me back.

Why?

It's the unanswerable question.

Maybe it was because she always had faith in our future, regardless of the hell we were in.

Maybe it was because she had known me in the age of innocence.

Maybe it was because she had two little kids and she was always putting out fires—her life in free-fall around her—and in some twisted way it was easier for her when I was around, as fucked up as I was. Two little kids and a job, too, first as a waitress in a Newport restaurant, then on the desk at a hotel.

Maybe it was as simple as love, the proof of which was all over the house: the pictures of us in happier times, the wedding picture in the living room, constant reminders of what we had lost.

Maybe it was all of the above.

Heather had seen my life crumble, its slow demise. Because addiction doesn't destroy you overnight; it's a slow walk down a tortuous hill.

Whatever the reason, I was back in the house and we quickly fell back into the same nightmare.

I couldn't think rationally. The money was all gone, and

you're a prisoner in your own body. You're constantly sweating. You're always breaking hearts. One time Heather and I went to Atlanta for a couple of days for a wedding. After two days I'm out of drugs, and I can't go searching for them because Heather's with me, and now I'm tired, sick, miserable, and just want to get the fuck out of there. I had sweated through my suit jacket.

Your life is scheduled around drug dealers. When are they going to be there? Can you get the money? And what happens if you can't? So I had two or three dealers, in case I couldn't find one. Or else I'd go into Fall River, where even a blind man could find drugs. The dealers have runners, and they know where the dealers are. All you had to do was go to South Main Street, drive slow, and just nod. That's all it took.

Just nod.

■CHAPTER THIRTEEN■

I had no job.

I had no money.

I had no hope.

I had no future.

I just had schemes to get through the day.

It was the summer of 2007, I was back from California, back in the house in Portsmouth, which by now we had sold to Heather's father, and I was a mean, nasty, angry drunk, in addition to being a heroin addict. I was in a constant blackout, shoveling down two or three pints of vodka a day. It was all shame, guilt, fear, anxiety, you name it.

It was vodka in the morning, heroin at lunch, vodka after dinner.

That was life in that last year.

The jig had been up a long time ago, of course, but when you run out of money the jig is really up. That's when you start living hard, and living hard isn't pretty. There's no hiding living hard. People recognize it.

How could they not?

I'm poking myself in the arm every day, sometimes five, six times a day. Every day I'm putting junk in my arm. Talk about despair. That's the definition of despair. It's like picking up a revolver to play Russian roulette five times a day. One bad shot from that needle and your life is over. I'm not sitting there when they're mixing that shit together. I don't know what's in it. I have no idea. And no one likes sticking needles into themselves. But that's the world you're in, a world of misery and pain and shattered lives.

That's the power of heroin.

The power of addiction.

If someone strapped you in a chair and did these things to you on a daily basis you would murder them. Instead, you're doing these things to yourself.

And when you're living like that you're way beyond the big picture.

Without basketball the bottom fell out. Basketball and money had merely prolonged the inevitable. Take the cash out and it's a whole new game. The grind really begins. With money there's no dope sickness, no panic. Without it, it's all panic, a constant panic.

And it affects everyone you come into contact with. Heather became as engulfed in it as I did. It became her world, too. She became ill herself. She lived every bit of my addiction, except she didn't buy it, and she didn't use it. But it dragged her down too, because that's what addiction does, it drags everyone down.

A friend helped me get a job at the Institute for International Sport at the University of Rhode Island. It was in Kingston, about forty-five minutes away, but my driver's license was suspended, so to get there I had to take a bus to Newport, wait around, then take another bus to Kingston. The institute was run by Dan Doyle, and he was throwing me a lifeline. A guy named Jerry Creamer, a retired high school principal and coach, was wonderful with me. He'd often drive me home to Portsmouth after work, even though it was completely out of his way. He wanted to help me. The institute did many incredible things, including putting on the World Scholar-Athlete Games, and in the beginning I was so desperate for a job I would have swept the floors. But I was so far down the sinkhole of my addiction that, ultimately, I couldn't do it, couldn't do anything.

How could I be at work when my real work was getting high every day? That was the only way I now knew how to live.

The institute also runs the New England Basketball Hall of Fame, and they wanted to put me in it, but I couldn't even handle that.

Talk about not being able to see the big picture.

In the end I stopped showing up; another bridge burned, more running from people who were trying to help me.

Everything was unraveling, completely out of control.

I had a succession of jobs for a while. I worked fixing houses for my cousin Ian. I did odd jobs for Andy Farrissey, who had been the huge Durfee star in 1947 when they first went to the Boston Garden for the championship game. I borrowed money from anyone who would lend it to me, telling them anything. But it was never enough.

We couldn't pay the bills. All the money was gone. The heat was turned off. Then we'd get the heat back on and the TV would be turned off. The TV would come back, and the lights would go off. That's how we lived in the winter of 2008, trying to keep a sinking ship afloat. Paying one bill, holding off on the others for as long as possible, until it's eventually too late and you're sitting there with no heat and it's the middle of the winter and the kids are wrapping themselves in blankets, and Heather's not speaking to me, and I know I have to do something, but what am I going to do, because if I don't somehow get to Fall River the next day I'm going to be in a fetal position, so sick I won't be able to move.

This is what it had come down to.

All the basketball fame and TV games. All the charter flights in the NBA and five-star hotels. All the cheers and all the appearances and all the newspaper headlines. All the money that came with that, all those big checks with big numbers on them.

And ultimately, maybe it was this simple: after all the autographs I signed and all the hands I shook, when it came time to call someone for a job, there was no one to call.

And Heather was pregnant.

She would go off to work in the morning and Sammy and I would go to the liquor store to get vodka before I put her on the bus and drove off to Fall River to chase down heroin, off into my own daily hell.

"Chris, I got your picture on my wall," some drug runner in the Fall River streets would say.

"I don't give a fuck about my picture on your wall. What do you got?"

"Chris, I went to your basketball camp," another kid would say.

"I don't give a fuck about that either."

At first they were starstruck, but I soon became just another junkie, just like any other sorry-looking dude on the street trying to score dope.

A guy I played basketball with as a kid sold me some Oxy-Contin one day.

"This is the last time I'm going to sell this to you," he said. "You're way out of control. You're ruining your life."

A lot of these people had gone to my games at Durfee, had rooted for me. And they didn't like seeing me like this. I could sense that. But I was way beyond caring.

There were stone-cold heroin addicts who said, "I can't be around this. I can't accept this. You're killing yourself."

I didn't stop.

As my world turned more and more hard-core, it got even more ugly. I was living in a deviant, dark, conniving, lying world.

A world where the conversation is all about who's in jail, and who died. Who's got the best dope. Who's got the worst dope.

How's so-and-so doing?

Not good.

How about so-and-so?

Not good.

These were the conversations.

You really don't have friends. Dope is your friend.

My only job, if you want to call it that, was driving a dealer around Fall River while he sold his junk. My payment? He gave me some, too. Because I no longer had the money to buy.

I was in a kitchen one morning and a woman was prostituting herself in the next room with the door open and her little kid could see it. I was with people who were sharing needles full of blood. I was in houses with no furniture, no TV, no anything, just mattresses on the floor, and little kids sitting on them. I saw things no one should ever see.

Hell couldn't be any worse.

On the night before I drove off the road in Fall River in front of the cemetery and was dead for thirty seconds, I went to a friend's house in South Kingstown. I was there for about an hour and then, as we walked down his driveway to where my car was parked, I threw up. I had been to his house before, but he explained to me how to get on Route 1 north, the road that would take me to the Newport Bridge and then back to Portsmouth.

It was very easy, just one turn.

I didn't take it.

About twenty minutes later I started seeing signs for Connecticut, which meant I had spent the last twenty minutes in a virtual blackout, going south when I should have been going north.

Is it any wonder that after another day of getting fucked up I don't remember driving through Fall River for a mile or so in the afternoon and passing out in the car with a needle in my arm, then being pronounced dead for nearly thirty seconds?

Hadn't I had this date for a long time?

■CHAPTER FOURTEEN■

Chris Mullin had arranged for me to go to Daytop, a rehab in upstate New York, and a car picked up Heather and me at the detox place in Fall River.

Daytop had been around since the late 1950s. It had been started in New York City by a young parish priest named William O'Brien, who began to realize that at the root of a lot of the street crime he encountered was drugs. He soon learned that there were few programs treating substance abuse, not with a whole lot of success, anyway.

Back then the attitude was "once an addict, always an addict," and neither jail time nor rehab would help. He found a program that did work in Connecticut, one that had been created by a recovering alcoholic and was based on both group encounters and addicts confronting each other. The first Daytop was opened on Staten Island in the early 1960s—it was called a therapeutic community—and it was a success. The first one in the Catskills opened in 1966.

I didn't know any of this, of course, when the car picked us up in Fall River. It was a three-and-a-half-hour ride, and it was a very difficult, emotional trip. There wasn't much to talk about. There was nothing to be solved. It had all been said. Heather was eight months pregnant, and for much of the ride she just lay across my chest. She was filled with mixed emotions. Pity. Sympathy. But love, too. A lot of love.

Rhinebeck, New York, is a small, artsy town in the Catskills, and Daytop is about three miles outside it. When we arrived there were guys with shovels and rakes outside, all working. The blue building looked like an old elementary school. It was mostly one floor, but part of it had a second floor, too.

A man named Larry came out to meet the car. He was a little Italian guy, mid-fifties, a Joe Pesci type.

Heather and I started to get out of the car.

"Where are you going?" he said to her.

"She's going to come in for a few minutes," I said.

"No she isn't," he said. "Give her a hug. She's got to go."

I was horrified.

I watched her drive away, not knowing what was going to happen. I didn't know whether she was going to stay with me, or when I'd see my kids again. They were all I had left, because everything else was gone.

I walked into the building and it seemed like chaos, everyone milling around.

They gave me a wooden chair and had me sit in a long hallway. There were eighty-two guys in the hallway, white, black,

Latino, and they were firing questions at me. Eventually, they told me to pick up the chair and take it to the end of the hallway, where the ritual was you were to place it down, sign your name, and wait to be called. After a while I was called into a tiny office. Five guys were there.

"What are you, a loser?"

"What makes you do the things you do?"

"What the fuck is the matter with you?"

They were confrontational, in my face. Later, I came to understand that they were trying to make sure that I wanted to be there, was willing to do what it took. I wasn't sure. I had absolutely no sense of who I was anymore, absolutely no confidence. That was all gone.

Their barrage lasted a few minutes, and I cried the entire time.

I was sweating and shaken.

I was completely broken.

"Welcome to Daytop," one of them finally said.

There were eight guys in my room, two white, ranging in age from twenty to sixty. Most of the men at Daytop had just come from prison, were in a transitional stage. The only other so-called volunteer was a guy in his sixties. Everyone was very supportive, very helpful.

The first two weeks were tough for me. I was still dope sick. There were no TVs. No radios. Lights were out at ten o'clock. You could make a two-minute phone call twice a day, but there were a lot of rules, and if you broke one of them, the first thing that went was your phone privileges. You could get busted for almost anything. Your bedsheet wasn't tight enough. Your shirt was out. You gave someone a bad look. Anything. At any time someone could get right in your face about anything, and if you got aggressive or confrontational you would be sent to COD, code for the "Chief of Duty."

I was put on maintenance, which meant all the shit jobs—washing floors, scrubbing toilets; all the jobs no one else wanted to do.

After about twenty days I began to feel better.

After about forty days Heather was ready to give birth.

Would I be allowed to go home for it?

That was the question, and like everything it was a communal decision, for at Daytop the inmates ran the asylum, at least in theory.

"Is he going to be able to go?"

"Do you think he can handle it?"

"I don't think he's ready."

On and on it went, everyone with an opinion. Eventually, I was allowed to go.

I was accompanied by Sean Boogs, another patient. He was twenty-six, had been in jail, and his job was to look out for me, make sure I didn't fuck up. We took the train to New York City, then another one to Providence. Heather and the kids met me at the station and we all went next door to the Providence Place Mall to get something to eat and let the kids play some video games.

Every time I went anywhere in the next couple of days, Sean went with me, into stores, the bathroom, everywhere.

Except once.

On the second day, we went to a pharmacy on West Main Road in Middletown, just a few miles from my house. There was a liquor store in the back, but Sean didn't see it. He stayed in the car. I bought a pint of Popov, guzzled it, and stuck a couple more down my pants. When I got back to the car, he was asking me questions, pressing me. He sensed that something was up. I had placed him in an unfortunate situation, but no one was going to stop me. That's how aggressive I could be.

Drew was born the next day by C-section, and I was a mess.

My face was breaking out. It was like the vodka was coming out of me.

"I'm staying one more day," I told Heather.

"No," she said. "You need to go back now."

I drank the other two pints and passed out in the car on the ride back to Daytop. I stumbled out of the car when we got there, smelling of alcohol. Letting me go home had been a test, and I had failed. And since alcohol always made me very aggressive, when a counselor came to get me, I lashed out at him.

"I'll break your jaw," I said to him.

I went inside and was put in the hallway in front of everyone again, all eighty-two of them. But this time I knew the drill. When you've fucked up, everyone has to decide if you get another chance or if you're out.

So I had to sit there while they decided my fate.

I sat in that chair in the hallway from eight at night until the next afternoon.

I was a complete mess.

I was thirty-two years old, I had three kids, and I was crying in the Catskills.

Then everyone started in on me.

"Chris fucked up."

"Chris is a wolf in sheep's clothing."

"Chris is always going to be a fuckup."

On and on it went, the same drum being pounded over and over again.

"Chris is fucked up."

"Chris is always going to be a fuckup."

Then Larry, the Joe Pesci guy, said, "Why don't you do the only noble thing you've ever done in your life and get away from your kids? Do them a favor and get the fuck out of their lives. Because you're like a ball and chain around their necks and they'll be better off without you. They'll be better off with any stepdad they end up with rather than you. Give them a break and get as far away from them as possible. Do them a favor and get out of their lives, because with you in their lives they have no fuckin' shot."

I believed him.

I lay in bed that night in total agony, and thought it probably would be better to get away from my kids. Maybe the best thing I could do was to give Heather a chance to have a normal life, to just get away and let the kids have a chance. Maybe that really was the most noble thing to do.

They say you have to find your bottom, whatever that is.

That night was my bottom.

It wasn't almost dying, as improbable as that might sound.

It certainly wasn't blowing all the money I made in basketball, though that's what so many people point to.

It wasn't the unbelievable shame, the kind of shame so powerful that you can't even look the people you care about in the eye.

It wasn't even the thought of losing Heather, this woman who has always been the love of my life, and without whose support I'm convinced I'd now be dead.

It was the idea that I would never see my kids grow up, would never again be in their lives in a meaningful way.

That was my bottom.

Because somewhere in the middle of the night, as I lay there thinking my world had ended, in the most despair I had ever felt in what had been years of despair, at the very bottom of this long journey through my personal hell, I had a flash of something. Call it a spiritual awakening. Call it God. Call it anything you want. But somewhere in the middle of that dark night, I knew I wasn't going to walk away.

I wasn't going to walk away from my kids.

I was going to be their dad.

I was put on something called "pot sink," which meant I had to wash all the dishes of eighty-two people three times a day. It was a very small space, about the size of a jail cell. It was blistering hot, no air, so you essentially were soaking wet all day long.

More important, I had lost all control.

No phone privileges.

No getting through to Heather.

No begging for forgiveness.

No trying to spin it.

I was in this small place by myself for eighteen days straight, Heather had just had a C-section and was home with three kids, and there was nothing pretty about any of it.

Heather would call my counselor, but she couldn't call me. She called him all the time.

"You know, Chris, she might not come back to you," the counselor said one day. "She's getting better."

I wanted to kill him. In my twisted mind I figured that if she worked on herself and got better, then she'd be done with me, that the only thing keeping her with me was that she had been so dragged down that she didn't see any way out either.

And it's just me all day in this little room that's screaming hot, continually washing dishes.

No group to go to.

No counseling.

No phone privileges.

It's just you.

You've got to figure it out.

No one else.

And the only thing you can do is think.

But for the first time in a long, long time I was sober and I had the time to think. How Chris has to learn how to be a father.

How Chris has to learn how to be a husband. How Chris has to learn how to be a person. How Chris has to learn how to live in the world.

No cell phones.

No drug dealers.

Nobody.

Just me and my own head.

I was right where I was supposed to be.

And what were the most important things running around in my head all day in that little kitchen?

What I had done to the people who loved me.

It wasn't what I had done to my basketball career, or how much money I had blown. That was irrelevant. I couldn't have cared less about that. It wasn't the shame I felt when I saw people who had known me before my addiction. It was the pain and complete agony I had put the people who loved me through. And I couldn't call Heather and say "I love you" or "Forgive me" or "Let's put this behind us," all those things that had worked so many times before. I was by myself, just me and all the thoughts constantly running through my head.

"Your marriage might be done," my counselor said, "and you're going to have to prepare yourself for that."

"I'm leaving," I said, wanting to run. "I'm going home."

That was my first response. The second? If my marriage was really going to end, then I had to get better so I could be a father.

So I prayed for Chris and Samantha.

I prayed for baby Drew.

I prayed for my marriage.

I prayed for my sobriety.

This lasted twenty-two days.

I ran it through my head all the time, like some newsreel. All the damage I had done. All the trust I had smashed. All the wreckage I had caused. The incredible guilt I had about all of it.

People at Daytop told me I had to get through all that guilt, that I couldn't keep beating myself up.

This is what the counseling did, what the groups did. You heard stories of people who had done it, and you began to realize you might be able to do it, too. But first you had to give yourself a break. You had to realize what you were, and that you could get through it one day at a time.

Because once you've been broken, once you're on the other side of the lies and the self-deception, once you've come to realize that you can't do it by yourself, they start to build you up.

You become a hall monitor. You wear a shirt and tie. Your responsibility is to keep the house in order, you and seven others. I did that for thirty days. Then I was put in charge of construction.

"I don't even know what a screwdriver is," I said.

"You're good with people," the counselor said. "Figure it out."

I had written Heather letters all along. In the beginning they often were about the guilt I felt. How I had become a burden to her. How I was a very sick person. How I was heartbroken and would be forever guilty. How I was so very scared.

One day I wrote her a letter saying how I had seen a sign that said, "If you were a child, would you look up to you?"

I went back to my room and cried like a baby after that.

Look up to me?

I'd be the last person I would look up to.

But eventually that became my goal: to be the kind of person my children could look up to.

I had been there for nearly four months when Heather and the kids came for their first visit. She drove three and a half hours in a van.

Heather and I met with a counselor. The kids were playing outside.

That night I was allowed to go to the hotel for a while. Heather and I watched the kids swim in the pool. We ate a meal as a family. And on the way back to Daytop, I thought of how blessed I was. To be able to eat dinner with my family when I was sober, not hiding vodka bottles. To be able to engage in conversation like a normal person.

That's what Daytop had done for me.

And when they left, I knew I had to be someplace closer. Daytop had been an amazing beginning. The people there had big hearts. There were always people there to help you. They had done so much for me, had taught me that you only start to get better when you're finally willing to admit the truth, that you're only as sick as your secrets.

I was beginning to understand addiction, how much of it is the refusal to deal with what is really going on, the self-deception that becomes so much a part of it.

I drink, smoke a little weed, but everybody does that, right?

I drink, smoke a little weed, blow some lines once in a while, but it's all under control.

I drink, do some weed, do some Ecstasy and some pills, but not all the time.

I do a little heroin, but I don't shoot it.

I shoot heroin, but there are a lot of people a lot worse than me.

I'm a junkie, but I've never been arrested.

These had been my crutches along the way, however foolish and pathetic they now seemed, as if you're really not that bad as long as there are people worse than you. That's the trap you fall into. And I hadn't just fallen into that trap, I had jumped into it.

They say the three things that being a junkie leads to are jail, institutions, and death.

Well, I'd been to jail, I was now in an institution, and I'd overdosed four times.

I had cheated death.

But now I had been at Daytop for over four months, I was sober, and I was ready for the next step, whatever that was.

Was Heather going to stay with me, or was she going to leave?

I didn't know.

But I knew I wasn't going to be here in the Catskills the rest of my life, knew it was time for the next act, whatever that was going to be.

And I knew I had to get back home.

———

I didn't go home.

But I got closer.

I was sent to Gosnold, a treatment center in Falmouth, Massachusetts, on Cape Cod, and assigned to Miller House, a halfway house. Just a couple of miles away was Woods Hole, a beautiful little village surrounded by water on three sides, where the boat to Martha's Vineyard leaves from. Miller House was an old Victorian, and the rules were that you went to twelve-step meetings twice a day. There were thirty guys living there, all ages.

Kevin Mikolazyk, who had taken his own to-hell-and-back journey since he had been in Fresno with me, was living on the Cape and had arranged it for me. He had stayed in California after I left, and it hadn't gone well. His addiction had caught up with him, too, and he had spent time in jail. But now he was four years sober, he was living in Falmouth, and he had connections with Gosnold.

The first thing you did in the morning at Miller House was pile into a white van with fourteen other guys and go to meetings, which were in the basement of a church in the middle of Falmouth.

In the beginning I never said a word.

I didn't want to take the first step, didn't want anyone to see that I was scared.

A few days later a woman named Mary, in her late forties, approached me.

"How are we going to get to know you, and how are we going to get a chance to love you, if you never say a word?" she said.

That was a turning point.

After that I started to talk. I talked about my kids. I never talked about basketball, or the Celtics, or any of that.

Eventually a woman approached me.

"Is it true that you played for the Celtics?" she asked.

I still didn't want to talk about it.

After the meeting we'd all pile back into the white van and go back to Miller House and meet in groups. Then we'd hang out for a while, maybe attend another group meeting in the afternoon and then go back into town for another meeting at night. These meetings were different, full of people who knew me, or whom I knew. Guys I grew up with. Guys who grew up with my brother. It sometimes seemed as if half of Fall River had ended up on the Cape. But there was a difference. These guys dressed well, had jobs. After the meeting these guys were going back to their families, their lives. I was going back to Miller House. I felt like a fuckin' animal, being herded into the white van every night. I started to feel sorry for myself.

Kevin quickly knocked that out of me.

"Be grateful for that white van, Chris," he said, "because that van takes you back and forth to meetings every day. That van is your lifeline."

After that I started to feel better. I stopped pitying myself. I had people I could talk with. I began to feel grateful.

After about a month, they let me get a job.

Mine was repossessing cars, and I got that, too, from Kevin.

Kevin was in real estate, but he also repossessed cars, along with his wife-to-be, Joleena. Business was good. The economy in Massachusetts had gone bust just as it had everywhere else, and there was plenty of work. It seemed that everyone was behind in their payments, so ours was a boom business in a bad time. Most of the time I rode with Joleena. She was an angel. She was twenty-seven, in recovery, too, and the time I spent with her was therapeutic. We would ride around talking about everything. I also was making a little money, and that was good, both for my self-esteem, which was rock bottom, and because Heather needed all the money I could send her.

In a sense, it was the first real job I'd ever had, one that had nothing to do with basketball. We were like bounty hunters. I got $50 a car, and I only had one rule. I wouldn't repossess a car that had car seats in it, and I wouldn't repossess vans, because they both meant kids. I had had my car repossessed in California, and I was sensitive to the consequences. But it was a job, and I needed one. Some days we'd ride around for twelve hours and only get one car, but Joleena would always pay me for two, because she knew how desperate I was for money. Joleena had a big heart.

I was knocking on people's doors, pulling cars out of people's driveways, and it was never easy for me. I knew that for 60 percent of the people losing their cars, it was because of substance abuse. Those were the ones that could break your heart. The others I had no problem with.

"It's a job," Joleena told me. "If it's not you, it's going to be someone else. And you have bills to pay."

The plan was to go home for Halloween for a night. It had been approved by a counselor.

But shortly before I was to leave, the director called me into his office.

"Christopher," he said, "we made a decision not to allow you to stay overnight."

I flipped.

"This is bullshit. I'm not a child," I said, storming out of the room.

Five minutes later I went back and apologized.

"We've been there, Chris," the director said. "You've got to trust us."

It was only the second time I'd been home in five months, and things had changed. Heather's father was now living in the house. Heather was essentially on welfare, on food stamps. She was making $420 a week and she was a single mother with three kids and a husband who was in a halfway house on the Cape. It wasn't easy.

I took the kids around the neighborhood that night in their costumes, one of the most normal things a father can do, but I was uncomfortable being back, tense.

I felt like an outcast.

I felt like a criminal.

I felt like a drug addict.

I felt like everyone was watching me, judging, whispering, talking about me once they closed the door.

The director had been right. I really wasn't ready to stay over-night. I was too raw.

Could I ever go back home and put this all back together, all these pieces that had been shattered?

I wasn't sure.

Did Heather want me back?

I thought so, but I wasn't sure of that either.

So much had happened, none of it good. Most people would have been out of that marriage four years earlier. For the first time, I had real doubts that she wanted to try again with me.

Who could have blamed her?

I thought about just staying on the Cape, away from Fall River and Portsmouth, places where there was too much bad history and too many people who knew too much. Would I ever be able to get past the shame? I didn't know. Staying on the Cape and starting over there seemed much easier. I was getting to know people through meetings, hearing about opportunities, and there were a lot of times when staying made the most sense to me.

Joleena and I would talk for hours, and all that helped me. With both her and Kevin I was seeing people who had been where I had been. No hope. No future. And no confidence that that was ever going to change. Yet they had resurrected them-selves, built new lives. In many ways they were my role models. They were a daily reminder that it could be done.

It was all about small victories.

One day I repoed a car and there were two pints of vodka in the glove compartment. It freaked me out.

"Get that out of here," I said to Joleena.

But that was a small victory, resisting the first real temptation. I could have grabbed the bottles and no one would have known. The meetings were small victories, too; anther day sober, another day of being vigilant. And the more I went to meetings in Falmouth, the more people I knew. There were five other guys from my era at Durfee going to meetings in Falmouth then, as drugs had swept through Fall River in the past decade like some invading army. Two of them I had played with in high school. That made it easier, along with Kevin and Joleena.

And things were getting better at home.

Heather and I could have a dialogue now. She was open to it. I was contributing some money, so things were easier. It wasn't just her against the world anymore. She saw that I was better, and believed that we could get back what we had lost. That was a huge step on my road to recovery.

One day a guy drove up the driveway of Miller House in a Cadillac. Some guys were shooting baskets in back of the house. They were always trying to get me to play, but I never did.

"Are you Chris?" the guy asked.

He was older, had that look of success about him.

"How are you making out?" he asked.

"I'm hanging in there."

He put $20 in my pocket.

"I know what you're going through," he said.

His name was Mike Fleming, and he ran a sober house, also in Falmouth. I lived there for a while after my health insurance refused to pay for Miller House anymore. Mike and I became great friends; he became part of my circle. And that was the thing: my circle was growing, little by little. I no longer felt I was shipwrecked on some private island, all alone with nowhere to turn. I had people who cared about me. I had people who had forgiven me. I had people who were starting to believe in me.

Miller House was the best thing I ever did. It gave me my confidence back. It made me realize I could face the world again, could go on in life. It made me start to forgive myself. Maybe most of all, it showed me that I had things to offer people.

It was time to go home.

■CHAPTER FIFTEEN■

The game changed on May 31, 2009.

At least publicly.

It was the lead story in the *Boston Globe* sports section.

The headline said in big, bold, type, "Changing of a Guard," and the subhead was "Finally clean and sober, Herren ready to embrace his post-basketball life."

There was a huge picture of me that dominated the front page.

It had me standing inside the field house at Durfee in jeans, sneakers, and a dark short-sleeve shirt, arms crossed, one foot on a basketball. Behind me were two banners. One listed the eleven one-thousand-point scorers in Durfee history. The other listed the two-thousand-point club: "Chris Herren, 2073 points, 1994."

The article was written by Marc Spears, who had covered the Nuggets for the *Denver Post* the year I was in Denver. We had run into each other at a Celtics play-off game I had taken Chris to.

The article started by saying that any chance of playing pro basketball anywhere in the world was now basically dead for me. I had a wife and three kids to support, and was seeking employment in tough economic times. But considering the long fight I'd had with alcohol and drugs, my current issues were "far from the end of the world."

"I've been to hell and back," I was quoted as saying. "I lived the life most people, a lot of people, don't get a chance to come out of, straight up. By the grace of God and the help from a plethora of people, I was able to come out of this."

I had gone home right before Christmas 2008, six months after crashing my car in Fall River, the symbolic fall. I had been to a detox facility, a rehab, and a halfway house, cried a million tears, stared endlessly into the abyss that my life had become, buried my mother on heroin, and almost lost my family. Somehow I had survived all of it.

Now we were starting again as a family, and from the minute I got home I knew it was going to work. And one of the huge reasons was Heather's father, Ken Gray. There's not a kinder, more forgiving man on the planet than Ken Gray. When I went away, he moved in and basically took care of Heather and the kids. He paid the bills. He helped the kids with their homework. He was another adult presence in my kids' lives when they so desperately needed one. He did everything. Then he did more. And when I came back, he was completely welcoming and supportive. I can't put into words what he has done for me.

When I came back I still faced a mountain of legal issues.

Operating under the influence.

Heroin possession.

Reckless driving.

Not to mention still being on probation in Rhode Island from the 2004 arrest.

I had the possibility of jail time hanging over my head, and there was no way I could afford an attorney.

Enter my father.

He arranged for me to meet a lawyer named James Killoran, whose kids I had played against in high school.

"Christopher," he said, "I'm going to help you every way I can."

He led me to a lawyer named Joe Silvia, and he led me through the court system. Only this time I was sober.

My license was suspended for two years.

I got five years probation.

I am still in the court system.

But that article changed everything.

Until then, my reentry into the world had been gradual. It had been day-by-day, week-by-week. I had been lost for so long. When I first got home I just did what I was supposed to be doing. I had proved to myself that I could do the right thing, go to meetings, work on my marriage, my family. Maybe more important, I was extremely comfortable in my own skin, something that I hadn't felt in a long time. I felt more and more comfortable going out of the house. I didn't feel ashamed for people to see me. My kids were smiling. I took Chris to the

Celtics play-off game. I took Sammy to her soccer games. It's all about small victories, and I was having them all the time.

And I knew that Heather and I were going to be all right.

She had done everything when I was so sick. Working. Cleaning the house. Taking care of the kids, keeping things as normal as they could be with a father who wasn't there, either physically or emotionally. Making sure they did well in school. I would hear that all the time when I got back home, from people at their school, from people in the neighborhood, from everyone, how nice the kids were. How respectful. How amazing. And that was all Heather. She was the one who held it all together. She was the star.

I don't think I would be alive today without her.

In many ways she became like my parent those last couple of years, when I couldn't do anything for myself. I look back now and don't know how she did it. Not only was she in the middle of my nightmare, she was in her own. Living a life she never could have envisioned. She hadn't grown up in chaos and dysfunction. She had done well in school, had graduated from college. She had done everything right. And here she was in a situation that had turned into complete insanity.

Somehow, some way, she had kept the faith that we could survive all this.

Because if 50 percent of all marriages end in divorce, what do you think the percentage is for heroin addicts? That she stayed in this marriage after everything she was put through is a testament to her faith, and to the fact that her love withstood all of the hell. She had to fight her friends who told her to get away from me, to turn me loose. She had to fight her own family members, who were telling her to get out of it. She fought all that pressure. She turned her back on all of the shame and humiliation, and made a life for herself and our children.

But she knew I was sick, and her marriage vows about in sickness and in health?

She always believed in them.

In the *Boston Globe* it said how I was thinking of starting a basketball school. The next day I got a call from a Boston lawyer named Pat Sharkey. He asked me if I would work out his son, Joe, who played for Northfield Mount Hermon. We worked out at a couple of places, at a home gym in Raynham, Massachusetts, and at the Bank Street Armory in Fall River. The Bank Street Armory was over a hundred years old, and the gym is right out of *Hoosiers*. My father played there when he was at Durfee, and I worked out there a lot the summer before I went to the NBA. It was the very definition of old-school: no air-conditioning, the kind of place where you felt you were really paying your dues.

The word started to get out, and Lauren Fiola, whose father, Ken, had been a huge Durfee star before Michael's time, was my second client.

The third was Andrew Chrabascz, who had just finished his freshman year at Portsmouth High School and was already a high school star. Andrew was about six foot six, and his father, who had played at Penn State, is six foot eight. One day his father brought him to the Bank Street Armory.

"You can probably teach him more than I can," I said to him.

"I just want you to teach him like you'd teach anyone else," he said.

More people were hearing about what I was doing, and I knew I needed a gym in Portsmouth, because I wasn't going to have a driver's license for the next two years.

But where?

There were a couple of places that said no, and then I got a meeting with the principal of Saint Philomena, a Catholic elementary school across the street from Portsmouth Abbey, less than two miles from my house. Her name is Donna Glavin. She asked me some questions, then she said: "We're a Christian school, and we believe in second chances. So I'm willing to let you use the gym."

She's another one of my heroes.

But would enough kids come?

More important, would parents let their kids come?

Because I knew that there were people who wouldn't sign on because of my past. That's just reality. To this day, it's the parents who have the biggest problem with it, not the kids, and I understand that. There are people who don't want to be around me because I was a drug addict, until one of their family members has a problem, and then I'm the first person they call.

One day, shortly after "Hoop Dreams with Chris Herren" opened, I got a call from a parent.

"Jocelyn wants to ask you a question," she said.

Jocelyn was her daughter, twelve years old.

"You're my hero. Would you come to my school with me on Hero Day?" Jocelyn asked me.

She wanted to present me to her class because I had been so positive with her in the gym.

Two other kids asked me to sponsor them at their confirmations.

I'll never forget these things.

I'll never forget Katie McDonald, whose picture had been on the front page of the Fall River *Herald News* with me when she was seven years old. Now she had torn her ACL on the day she had signed a college scholarship, and we began helping each other back, her rehabbing her knee and me proving to myself that I could help kids.

They were big victories, proof that I could impact kids' lives.

As the word quickly spread, kids came to the basketball school. And what do they know about my past?

They know it all.

Google me and it's all there. There's no hiding anything in today's world. It's as close as a click on a computer.

And what they don't know, someone will tell them.

But it's how I treat them on a daily basis that's important. That's what they care about. They don't care about the other stuff. It's irrelevant to them. They care about my basketball story, not my addiction story. Most of all, they care about how I treat them.

And I treat them all differently.

It depends on what kind of household they're coming out of.

Some kids need to be pushed, encouraged to be more aggressive. If they have an aggressive father, or parents who are putting pressure on them, I back off. Some kids are growing up under tremendous parental expectations, in high-stress situations, and they remind me of myself at that age. I'm very sensitive to that, to trying to reduce the stress level. It's not basketball that breaks kids down. It's parents.

I have kids who drink too much, others who smoke pot. They see it as no big deal, the way I saw it at their age. To them, I hope I'm a cautionary tale. But I get to know about their lives, about their schools. More important, I get to know about their self-esteem. That's the most important thing. Because basketball is a short ride for all of us, regardless of how far we go in the game.

Basketball ends.

People ask me how I deal with blowing my basketball career, the years I could have been in the NBA, the money I could have made.

And you know what I tell them?

If I was still playing basketball, maybe I wouldn't even be alive now. Maybe I would have been found dead in some lonely hotel room in some foreign country, because that was the path I was on. Maybe I would have gotten arrested again and wound up with a jail sentence. Maybe I wouldn't be around as much, wouldn't be as totally involved in my kids' lives as I am now. I know I wouldn't be dealing with kids and helping them get to college, or play for their high school teams. I know I wouldn't have the tremendous satisfaction of getting to know the kids I now deal with, to be a meaningful part of their lives, if only for a little while. I always knew I wanted to deal with kids someday. Well, that day is now.

I know I am where I'm supposed to be.

I have a kid who called me at two in the morning in tears, his world moving way too fast, to tell me he had a serious drug problem and ask if I could help him.

I have a kid whose mother just committed suicide, and one day I could see he was struggling. We went outside for about a half hour.

"First of all," I said, "your mother's in a better place. And you know what? I'm in the same situation you are. My mother died too young, too. But I am closer to her now than I was when she was alive. I know she's here with me. And your mother's here with you, too. Everything happens for a reason. And maybe this is why you ended up here with me; maybe that's all part of God's plan."

Because I've come to believe there's a big spiritual component in my life.

I get on my knees and pray every morning. I get on my knees and pray every night.

Why do I pray?

Because I was at a meeting one night that sticks with me.

"Do you know why I pray?" an older man said. "Because every day I ask the good Lord to help me not to drink and I haven't drank yet. So someone up there must be listening."

That's good enough for me.

It's really not about the basketball.

It's about all the things you can learn from basketball.

At my camps there are only four rules: encourage each other, no bullying, no laughing at one another, don't make anyone feel less than you are.

I want kids to have a good memory of the camp, even the chunky kid with glasses who is probably never going to make his high school team. That kid may never play basketball again, but he can learn the game, learn what being on a team means, learn something about basketball. He can have a great experience.

I also pretend that every kid has a difficult home situation, even if they don't.

I know how fragile kids can be.

Chris is now eleven and plays on an AAU team. One day last spring Heather was taking him to Boston to play against a very good team from Boston, all inner-city kids. Michael was following them in another car.

Heather called me.

"Chris is having a breakdown," she said. "He doesn't want to play."

I called Michael, told him the deal.

When he got there he took Chris aside.

"I don't care two shits about how many points you score, or how many turnovers you have," Michael said to him. "I just want to see you run around and have fun."

I think everyone sees the big picture in all of this now—my father, Michael, all of us. We all know we paid a price for the way we were raised with basketball. But nobody needs to feel guilty for it, or apologize for it. When my father first put the ball in the hands of Michael and me, he didn't know what was going to happen, didn't know how any of this was going to play out. I don't need an explanation. I have made my peace with it. It's resolved in my own head.

Heather also sees the big picture. Then again, she grew up with me.

She knows.

I never walked across the lines of a basketball court in my life without feeling stress, and there's no way I'm going to let that happen to my kids. My message to Chris is very simple: you only play if you like it. If you don't, go do something else. I try not to put any pressure on him, because he has enough on him already, being named Chris Herren. And when I sense that he's feeling pressure, I nip it in the bud. He had an AAU tournament last spring at the Reggie Lewis Center in Boston, and before the game he said he had a stomachache. I knew what that was, and I told him that if playing AAU was going to make him tense and anxious, then forget about it, he wasn't going to play. I don't want my kid crying over a silly round ball.

I think today's basketball culture can be very detrimental to kids.

The days of playing in your buddy's backyard are over. There's no playing just for fun. No one plays two sports anymore, never mind three. It's all changed for the worse.

Some fifteen-year-old kid plays in an AAU tournament and

his game is instantly evaluated on some Web site, and he's labeled. Can play. Can't play. What's that all about, evaluating fifteen-year-olds? What good does it do for some kid to hear that he's never going to play in college? What good does it do to have his dreams shattered at fifteen? What have we created? When I was a kid, someone like Bob Gibbons might evaluate the top recruits every couple of months, and that was in a publication. Now kids are evaluated after every AAU game, it's all over the Internet, and I have parents who want to kill the guys who write about their kid.

Now kids are recruited to go to prep school because college coaches won't go into their high school gyms to see them play. Now everyone wants a college scholarship because kids know that the economics of college are ridiculous, and too many kids feel that if they don't get a scholarship they've failed their family. Now too many kids are growing up trying to make their father's dreams come true, feeling too much pressure. It's way over the top.

You know how sports should be judged?

If your kids are smiling when they're playing, then they are a success.

That's what matters.

Nothing else.

One of the other immediate results of the *Boston Globe* article was that I got a call from a woman who asked if I would talk to her son. He had a serious drug problem, and was off at a private school for kids with substance abuse issues. From the beginning I knew I could help him. I had been there. I could talk his language. That was the start of speaking to kids about the danger of drugs, how they have the power to take everything away from you: your hopes, your dreams, all the things you hold most dear in the world. Drugs are a game you're not going to win.

I do a lot of that now. I speak at schools. I speak at basketball camps. I tell my story, and I don't leave anything out. Who knows how many kids hear it? When I was their age, I wouldn't have. But you never know. And they have to hear it. Let's see, they have a basketball camp where they deal with basketball all day long for a week, and they deal with substance abuse, which runs like a fast break through every high school in the country, for maybe a half hour. Does that make any sense?

I know from dealing with kids that many of them have issues, some that are being dealt with, some that are not. I also know that substance abuse is a huge problem with kids, more than most people realize, because I'm around kids all the time and I hear the stories.

One day I was speaking at a basketball camp and this is how the guy introduced me:

"Raise your hand if you scored a thousand points in high school."

"Raise your hand if you scored two thousand points in high school.

"Raise your hand if you were a McDonald's All-American."

"Raise your hand if you played in the NBA."

That gets their attention.

And when I speak, I can see the one kid who nods his head, and the one that doesn't want to look at me. I see the ones who look bored, and the ones who just stare. Who knows what they're thinking? But they have to hear it, because I have learned that addiction isn't just my story, but a huge story out there that affects countless people, and I have the potential to help some of them. And I've come to see this as a gift; I know I can help people.

In the fall of 2009 I was hired by Gosnold as a community relations consultant. Essentially, I do whatever they ask me to do, whether it's to speak at functions, help with fund-raisers, whatever. Gosnold has been amazing to me. It was the place that got me sober, the place that's opened doors for me. Ray Tamasi, the president, has been wonderful, and it's a privilege to be able to help people, to be part of that process. I'm constantly trying to get people in, because I get countless calls and e-mails asking for my help. And I know what they're feeling, the shame, the guilt, the hopelessness. I also know that just by asking for help, they have taken a huge step.

When I speak to groups, my message is always the same.

No one sets out to be an addict. No one sets out to ruin their life and the lives of all the people around them. No one sets out to see the anguish in the eyes of the people who love them. No one sets out to live in constant chaos. No one sets out to live the life I led. It happens over time, sure. But it also happens when you don't address your issues.

Why do you feel the need to go out and get blasted every weekend when you're in high school?

Why do you feel you have to go through life loaded, numb?

Why do you continually deceive yourself, telling yourself you're not that bad, that there are many people worse than you and you can quit any time you really want to?

These are all the warning signs.

They are the ones I ignored, of course.

I had three visits with a drug counselor at Boston College, but I was nineteen years old and had blinders on. I wasn't looking for help. I remember at Boston College going to hear an ex–football player who had gone through substance abuse problems, and thinking I was never going to be thirty-five and like him.

I see that in kids all the time now. You look at them and know that unless they change their behavior they're heading for a big fall.

That's what I tell them.

I also tell them that I was never the most fucked-up kid in my circle of friends in high school, never the one who drank the most, or did the most drugs. That there were always kids worse off than me. I tell them that nobody would have predicted what was going to happen to me back then, the hell I would live in, the price I would pay for my addiction. I tell them that addiction is a sneaky thing, that it happens over time, until one day you wake up and you are your addiction. It owns you, not the other way around. I tell them that that's what happens when you don't deal with your issues.

And I tell them that I would give my left arm to have escaped all that.

Twice a month I speak at Star, the detox in Fall River I went to in June 2008, the one where I thought it was a good plan for someone's girlfriend to put some dope inside a tennis ball and throw it up to us on an outdoor patio. There are usually about fifty guys there, all Fall River guys, all guys who know who I am.

One night I told the story about stealing from my kids' piggy bank, and what an awful place in your head that is, to feel that desperate.

A guy raised his hand.

"I need to tell you something," he said.

He said how he had gotten back from Iraq and his life had fallen apart, and one night he, too, took money from his kid's piggy bank. He, too, had thought he was the only person who had ever fallen so low.

Afterward, he gave me a hug.

"I cried when you told that story," he said. "Thank you for telling it. I didn't think there was anyone else out there who had done what I did."

That's why meetings are so important. You have to hear people's stories over and over, get a daily reminder of the battle you are facing. You have to be constantly reminded that you're not alone, not the only one going through this. People have to believe that they can get out of their mess.

And I'm not saying I'm cured, or that I know all the answers. But I thank God for my ability to stay sober, and to be around people who are sober. People like Bob Eagan, one of the first guys in our group in Fall River to get sober. He has been a true support system for me, someone who understands addiction and is always there for me. I know what works for me: go to meetings. Let the past go, because to dwell on it only brings regret and guilt. Don't think about the future, because that brings fear. I just stay where I'm supposed to be. I know that if I stay in the moment and take care of my business, I have a chance.

Before the play-offs started in 2009, Austin Ainge, Danny's son, invited Chris and me to a Celtics practice in Waltham. So many guys were great to me that day. Paul Pierce. Ray Allen. Eddie House. Stephon Marbury. More important, they were great with Chris. They made a point to come over and meet him. Paul gave him a pair of his Nikes. For them to take the time for my son's sake was something I'll never forget. Chris was on cloud nine.

This was how Marc Spears's *Boston Globe* article about me ended:

"I don't need to validate anything. But for my kid growing up knowing that his father used to be a Celtic, and he had a chance to see that it was real. It wasn't just on the Internet and it wasn't just on trading cards.

"And when Paul handed him the shoes with 'To lil' Chris,' when my son walked away, it was priceless. That's the thing. There are bad memories, real bad memories. But over the last year there have been good ones."

I'm not haunted anymore about what might have happened in my career if my addiction didn't get in the way. I made choices in my life, and I live with them. To dwell on what might have been is all guilt and shame, and what's the point?

There is no point.

I feel blessed to have gotten my family back, to have gotten my life back. Blessed to be able to work with kids. My NBA career is just a blip on my radar screen; it means more to other people than it does to me. My career now, one that means so much more to me than my own basketball journey ever did, is to help as many kids as I can move through their own journeys.

But you know what?

I can help kids with their basketball experiences.

That's the beauty of it.

Because I have been where they're trying to go.

In the play-offs that year, Austin Ainge left Chris and me two tickets, good seats.

I had people coming up to me, welcoming me back. Chris was wearing his Ray Allen jersey, and I was taking pictures of him on my cell phone. It was huge. I was so happy to be there, right in the moment, enjoying everything about it.

And that night, for the first time, sitting underneath all those banners, in the midst of all that amazing history, I appreciated what I had done for the first time. It had never registered before.

It had meant nothing. There had been too much pain involved, too much absolute misery. Now I saw how amazing it had been. Chris Herren, a six-foot-two white kid from Fall River who had grown up in his driveway fantasizing that he was Larry Bird and Danny Ainge, just another little kid by himself dreaming all his basketball dreams, had actually seen them come true, and how many kids in this world can say that? I was a part of that unbelievable Celtics tradition, as small and insignificant as my role had been.

I had never felt that before.

All that had gotten by me, lost in the pain and misery of that year.

That night in 2009 I saw it all through my son's eyes, and for the first time I felt pride that I once played for the Celtics.

My kids also brought me back to Durfee basketball.

Chris and Samantha had come with me one day in the summer of 2009 to the Durfee basketball camp, and they were thrilled when they saw the banners on the wall with my name on them. They loved it. I had walked by that wall so many times in the past without seeing it, almost as if it didn't exist. That, too, had meant nothing, because I had lost my innocence a long time ago.

But now I was seeing it through their eyes, and it made me appreciate it in ways I never had before. Made me appreciate that my story was a basketball story, too, not just an addiction story, one that saw me overcome a zillion odds, get in magazines and on national television, live all over the world, and play in the biggest arenas in the country. A story that no one ever could have made up when I was just a kid in the Milliken League.

A story my kids could be proud of.

And I could be proud of it, too.

■EPILOGUE■

In May 2010 I was inducted into the Durfee Athletic Hall of Fame.

I had always been so conflicted about Durfee. What should have been such a great time had been far more complicated than that. My issues had gotten in the way even back then, to the point that much of my high school career had been painful, the last two years only half-remembered, a preview of things to come. It's what Jim O'Brien, my coach at Boston College, had said years before to the officials at Boston College when they didn't know what to make of me.

"Read *Fall River Dreams*. It's all in there."

I had focused on all the negative things. My guilt over the fights with Mr. Karam. The feeling of being in a fishbowl. The pressure I felt to be great. That I had to win for the city. The guilt over not winning the state championship.

This had become Durfee basketball to me, or at least my memory of it.

But I had come to see the other side, too.

When I almost died that June day in 2008 and was taken to the hospital with no health insurance, it was Bobby Karam, Mr. Karam's brother, who arranged for me to stay there. When Heather so desperately needed a job, it was Jimmy Karam, the third brother, who gave her a job at one of the hotels he owned. Mr. Karam showed up at my court appearances in Fall River. I saw the loyalty that surrounded Durfee basketball, the sense of brotherhood, the side I never had appreciated before, being so immersed in my own little world.

And I got a letter from Jeff Caron.

I was at Daytop, as low as I could possibly be, when his letter arrived. I was shocked. It was the only one I ever got there from anyone other than Heather, my father, and my brother.

Jeff and I had a complicated relationship at times. Basketball got in the way. It was always Jeff and me. We were the two best players in our class at Durfee. He had his own basketball dreams, and we both were very competitive, so it's only natural that there would have been times when he might have resented all the attention I got. Who wouldn't have? But we have an amazing history together. Our mothers were friends in high school, to the point that every time I see his mother now I want to cry, because I think of my mother.

I can remember playing basketball at his house when we were about ten. He had a hoop on a tree, and every time the ball went through the hoop it would bounce away. We spent more time chasing the ball than playing. We used to pretend we were

Duke and North Carolina and we would go at each other. But Jeff Caron was never the problem. I was the one with the problem. I was the one with the issues, not him.

In his letter he said that he knew what I was made of, and that he believed in me. He said he had no doubt that I could recover from this and get my life back. He also said that he was sorry he hadn't been there for me when I was having my problems, but he hadn't known what to say.

The letter came at a time when I felt such shame, such despair, when I thought there was no way I could ever go back to Fall River, when I felt like such a pariah. And here Jeff was telling me he believed in me, that he knew I could get my life back, and that he would be there for me. It meant the world.

That is why I wanted him to introduce me at the Durfee Hall of Fame dinner. He had gone on to play at Merrimack and had come back to be the coach of Durfee, before becoming the athletic director at Dartmouth High School, in a suburban town between Fall River and New Bedford. I knew that no one could introduce me any better. We had lived it all together, the good, the not so good, all of it. He had known me from the beginning. We had walked the same streets, played in the same games.

It was a wonderful night.

It was at the Venus de Milo restaurant in Swansea, Massachusetts, not far from Fall River, and in a symbolic sense it was my return to Fall River. I was finally the person that so many of the people in the room had always hoped I could be. It was also the first time I ever spoke of my addiction in front of my kids.

How much did they know?

I'm not naïve.

They knew something wasn't right, that's for sure. They knew when the lights were off. They knew when the TV was off. They knew when their parents were arguing. They knew when their father didn't live there anymore.

Chris had been old enough to know things. He could read the stuff on the Internet. His friends could read it. He knew. When I came home for the birth of Drew, after I had been in Daytop for a month, I took Chris and Sammy aside and told them that I loved them and that I was going to be home for good soon, and that they would never see me take another drink. I told them this, and by the end of it, we were all crying. Then two days later they saw me drinking.

They knew.

It was the thing I felt the most guilt about, that I had put them in situations they never should have been in. Chris waiting in the car in Fall River when he was just a little kid and I'd be inside some dealer's house in some shit neighborhood. Sammy in the backseat when I went to the liquor store in the morning in Portsmouth, then on the drug runs to Fall River before she got on the school bus. This is the guilt I'll always carry with me.

But I also know deep down in my heart that when all is said and done, what my kids so desperately wanted was for me to be back in the house and for us to be a family again. I see that every day. What they wanted was what all kids want, a dad who is there every day, a dad they can depend on. I see that every day, too.

I had nothing prepared when I went up to speak, no notes, no anything. If I couldn't talk about this, what could I talk about?

I knew I had to talk about my journey, that anything else would have been a sham. It had all been too public. It had been all over the Fall River *Herald News*—the arrests, the court appearances, all of it. Everyone in that room knew it anyway, at least the big, broad brush strokes of it. Yes, these people had known Chris Herren the basketball player. They had also known Chris Herren the drug addict. Many of these people had watched me grow up, supported me along the way, then had seen it all blow up. They deserved some closure, too.

So I talked about it.

But it was more difficult than I thought it was going to be.

Just off to my right, at the first couple of tables, were my family and some friends. And as I talked, I could see the tears rolling down their faces. Heather's. My father's. Michael's. My friends'. All were crying.

But not Chris and Samantha.

They were looking at me with big smiles on their faces.

And I knew then that they were going to be all right.

We all were going to be all right.